IVAN "IRONMAN" STEWART'S
ULTIMATE
OFF-ROAD ADVENTURE
GUIDE

Ivan Stewart
with Peter Economy

MOTORBOOKS

First published in 2007 by MBI Publishing Company LLC and Motorbooks, an imprint of MBI Publishing Company, Galtier Plaza, Suite 200, 380 Jackson Street, St. Paul, MN 55101 USA

Motorbooks titles are also available at discounts in bulk quantity for industrial or sales-promotional use. For details write to Special Sales Manager at MBI Publishing Company, Galtier Plaza, Suite 200, 380 Jackson Street, St. Paul, MN 55101 USA.

To find out more about our books, join us online at www.motorbooks.com.

Library of Congress Cataloging-in-Publication Data

Stewart, Ivan.
   Ivan "Ironman" Stewart's ultimate off-road adventure guide / by Ivan Stewart and Peter Economy.
      p. cm.
   ISBN-13: 978-0-7603-2926-9 (softbound)
   ISBN-10: 0-7603-2926-5 (softbound)
   1. Automobile racing—United States. 2. Off-road racing—United States. I. Economy, Peter. II. Title. III. Title: Ultimate off-road adventure guide.
   GV1033.S74 2007
   796.720973—dc22
                                        2007006138

Editors: Jennifer Bennett and Lee Klancher
Designer: Michael Cawcutt

Printed in China

On the cover: Toyota's FJ Cruiser makes for a great off-road vehicle.

On the back cover: Plan your best route and then execute it. But be prepared to adjust it quickly in the event that conditions are not as you anticipated. *Ken Brubaker*

On the frontispiece: Off-road travel adventure is all about new places, new people, and new perspectives.

On the title pages: The passes above Leadville, Colorado, offer some of the most scenic off-roading in the United States. This trail crosses the 13,185-foot-high Mosquito Pass. *Lee Klancher*

contents

Introduction 06

>> **PART I: BEFORE YOU GO** 07

ch_1: get ready for travel adventure 08
ch_2: what to bring 30
ch_3: the off-road adventurer's code 48

>> **PART II DRIVING SKILLS** 61

ch_4: the mental game 62
ch_5: basic off-road driving skills 76
ch_6: advanced off-road driving skills 98
ch_7: dirt and dust 110
ch_8: wet and water 118
ch_9: paved roads 124
ch_10: sand 134
ch_11: silt 140
ch_12: mud and muck 142
ch_13: rocks and boulders 148
ch_14: snow and ice 154
ch_15: up hills ... and down 160

>> **PART III ULTIMATE TRAVEL ADVENTURE DESTINATIONS** 165

ch_16: mike's sky ranch, baja 166
ch_17: gonzaga bay, baja 174
ch_18: moab, utah 178
ch_19: valley of fire state park, nevada 180
ch_20: assateague island, maryland/virginia .183
ch_21: ocala national forest, florida 184
ch_22: cape cod, massachusetts 186
ch_23: jeep jamboree 187
ch_24: the rubicon trail, california 188
        about the author 189
        index 190

As I look back over my life, it seems like I've been living one great big off-road adventure for much of it. I think I was born to race—off road. Other race car drivers like to drive in circles for hour after hour and mile after mile, others love to go hundreds of miles an hour straight down a quarter-mile track, then get pulled back to earth with a parachute. Others like the zigs and zags of road courses, where you go fast for a bit, then brake for a turn, then go fast, then brake again—over and over until the checkered flag waves down the finish. Me? I prefer the freedom of racing off road. Every day—and every night—brings with it new obstacles and challenges, as well as opportunities. Nothing is the same, and everything is different.

But accompanying those off-road obstacles and challenges is something my road-racing colleagues rarely experience: the shear beauty and majesty of a blood-red sun rising over a sandy playa, or the glow of a full moon illuminating 7,000-foot snow-covered mountain peaks. I have 84 career victories to my name, including 17 Baja 500 wins, 3 Baja 1000 wins, and 10 career driver's championships. Each one of these races was an adventure in the truest sense, and it's this spirit of adventure that I want to awaken within you as you read this book.

I have specifically designed this book to cover the topics that are most important to any prospective off-road adventurer, regardless of your level of experience. Whether you're an off-road beginner or a seasoned veteran, you'll find something new and useful in these pages. Plus, I have filled this book with some of my favorite personal stories from my many years of off-road adventure. And, let me tell you, I have been in some crazy situations in some very out-of-the-way places. I've loaded this book with priceless tips and advice that will provide you with everything you'll need to safely and easily plan and embark on your own off-road adventures. Believe me—you do not have to be an expert to have fun off road! And, as you'll soon find out, you don't even have to have a four-wheel drive vehicle. If you're looking for off-road travel adventure, then this book is your ticket to ride.

It is my personal hope that this book will inspire you to seek out your own adventures, while collecting tips and learning lessons that will ensure that your adventures will be safe and enjoyable. Nothing can compare to the experience of going off road. Every time you go, there will be something new around the next bend. Give it a try, and I think you'll agree, there's nothing quite like an off-road adventure.

Ivan Stewart
San Diego, California

BEFORE YOU GO

Embarking on an off-road travel adventure is one of the most fun and exciting things you'll ever do in your life. It's exactly that fun and excitement that got me started in my off-road racing career—and kept me there for so many years. But, before you go off road, you will need to prepare for the journey. In the following chapters, I explain how to prepare your vehicle and yourself for your off-road adventure. I'll tell you exactly what to bring along. I also describe the Off-Road Adventurer's Code—a set of rules that will help make your off-road adventure fun and enjoyable.

THE OFF-ROAD EXPERIENCE IS

AN ADVENTURE LIKE NO OTHER.

chapter 1

>>GET READY FOR TRAVEL ADVENTURE<<

The off-road experience is an adventure like no other. Maybe you're planning to storm the sand dunes in your 4x4 pickup truck or tow your bass boat to a secret fishing hole that's far off the beaten track. Maybe your plan is to take your RV on a camping trip in a remote forest—where all you'll hear is the wind blowing through the trees and the rustling of birds, squirrels, deer, and raccoons, and where you can watch the slow turning of the Milky Way as it spins around the North Star high above you. Or, maybe you are getting ready to go on a hunting or photographic expedition far up in the hills. Whatever the case, taking an off-road travel adventure is perhaps the easiest way to leave behind the hustle and bustle of your daily life, and get closer to nature and to the essence of who you really are.

In my many years of off-road racing and adventure travel, I've been to Baja so many times I've lost count, but I can tell you one thing: each time I go off road, I see things I've never seen before, I do things I've never done before, and I meet people I've never met before. For example, if you make it down to Baja, you might meet the legendary Coco, a fixture of the Baja 1000 ever since it began in 1967, whose compound (Coco's Corner) in the middle of the Baja desert between Gonzaga Bay and Bahía de los Ángeles can easily be picked out by NASA astronauts in space when he's got all his lights fired up.

To me, that's what off-roading is all about—exploring and experiencing something new. It's really true:

when you go off road, there's a new adventure waiting for you around every corner. Sometimes those adventures will take you to places you never imagined, sometimes they will make you smile, sometimes they will make you cry, and sometimes they will put you in awe of the sheer power and majesty of nature and of the world in which we live. You'll make memories that last a lifetime.

I'll never forget the time when Johnny Johnson, Frank Arciero Jr., and I were prerunning for the Baja 500—that is, driving the course before the race so we'd know what to watch out for. We were down in a very desolate part of Baja, north of San Felipe. It was

>> **Off-road adventures are some of the most memorable adventures you'll ever experience.** *Rick Shandley*

very hot, and we were out in the middle of nowhere. As we were driving down this long wash, we saw some movement ahead of us. Typically, if you see something moving around down there, it'll turn out to be a jackrabbit, a coyote, or maybe even a burro. As we got closer, we realized the movement we saw was actually three guys—all running around like red ants on a hot skillet.

The first question we asked ourselves was, "Why are these guys here, and why are they running around?" As we got closer, we had one more question: "Why are they naked?"

Frank thought maybe there was a canal out there and these guys were just going for a swim. Following that particular train of thought to its optimistic conclusion, Johnny suggested that maybe there were some girls out there too—and maybe they were skinny-dipping! I reminded them both that there were no canals in that part of Baja and that the possibility of anyone—man or woman—skinny-dipping in the area was very remote. After a quick discussion, we decided that we had probably encountered some locals who had smoked too much locoweed and that we'd better take a wide berth around them. No one with a shred of sanity runs around naked in the middle of the Baja desert—especially not in 110-degree heat.

As we got closer, the men flagged us down, and we figured we'd better stop to see if they needed help. It turned out that the day before, these guys were prerunning the race on motorcycles, missed a turn, and ran out of gas. They thought that when they got near a place called Tres Posos, there would be a sign pointing

>> **Great fishing spots can be found deep in the wilderness. This spot is just off the trail to Tin Cup Pass near Buena Vista, Colorado.** *Lee Klancher*

>> **The passes above Leadville, Colorado, offer some of the most scenic off-roading in the country. This trail crosses the 13,185-foot-high Mosquito Pass.** *Lee Klancher*

>>THERE'S SOMETHING SPECIAL ABOUT OFF-ROAD RACING<<

I'm often asked, "Why off-road racing? Why not drag racing or circle track or something else?" The reason I'm so fascinated with our sport is because in any other form of racing—for example, road racing—you're tied to a track. With drag racing, you're stuck to a drag strip. With Formula 1, you're stuck to a Formula 1 track. In off-road racing, however, there are no such constraints. We race on pavement, gravel roads, silt, sand, snow—anything you could ever imagine. We've even raced inside football stadiums. We could go to the Indianapolis 500 and race on the same track as the Indy cars, but we could also go into that beautiful infield golf course—say hole number 9—and jump a sand trap. I've always wanted to do that. The Indy guys can't do that, and neither can the NASCAR guys. We're not limited by anything—just our imaginations. To me, that's what makes racing fun.

the way to into town and the way to the highway. No dice, and missing the turn was their first mistake.

After the first guy ran out of gas, they pooled their remaining fuel and put it into one rider's tank so he could ride for help. That's when the group made their second mistake. The rider took the long way into town, and he ran out of gas, too. Fortunately, he was able to find his way back to the others. So these guys were stuck in the middle of nowhere—no gas, no water, no shade, and the very real possibility that no one would find them alive. As they later told us, the reason they took their clothes off was because it was the only way they could cool down. When we showed up, they were getting ready to attack a cactus to see if they could squeeze some drinking water out of it.

We gave them water and clothes and offered them a ride out—after they put on the clothes—which they gladly accepted. After we got them hydrated and calmed down, they told us their story. As it turned out, when the guy who went for help ran out of gas, it was nighttime and pitch dark. He was determined to get back to his friends, however, and he made it by walking all 10 miles back along the crown of the trail he rode out on—wearing his helmet. I asked him why he wore his helmet and he said, "There are coyotes out there—if I fell down and they attacked me, I didn't want them to chew my ears off."

I said, "You guys are running around naked and you're worried about your ears?"

>> **Although you can take a 2x4 vehicle off-road without too much worry, a 4x4 is usually the better choice.** *Rick Shandley*

I can't guarantee that every off-road journey you take will be quite as memorable as this one was for me, but you won't know until you get out there and find out. So, it doesn't matter why you're thinking about going on an off-road travel adventure, always remember that you're out there to do something new, to get closer to nature and the wide world around us, and, above all, to have fun.

THE ABCS OF OFF-ROADING

Before we get started, there are a few things you should know, such as some of the lingo that off-roaders use, that will make you more knowledgeable about your vehicle. This knowledge can go a long way toward increasing your fun factor in the process. First, let's consider two basic types of off-road vehicles:

- 4x4 (four by four): When you're thinking about going on an off-road adventure, chances are you're thinking about doing it in a 4x4 vehicle. As you may have already guessed, a 4x4 is any vehicle (car, truck, SUV, etc.) with four wheels that has power going to all four wheels. This makes your vehicle more effective in getting through

slippery, rocky, mushy, steep, or other challenging situations where you need maximum traction.

- 2x4 (two by four): Although more than a few people take 2x4 vehicles off road, a 4x4 is usually a much better choice. This is because while a 2x4 has four wheels, it only sends power to two of them. In the case of a rear-drive vehicle, power goes to the rear wheels; in the case of a front-drive vehicle, power goes to the front wheels.

Those are the basics. Of course, if you start digging deeper into the off-road world, you'll find that things get a bit more complicated pretty quickly. Such is the case with four-wheel drive (4WD) vehicles, which come in a variety of different flavors:

- Part-time 4WD: If you've got part-time 4WD, that means you have the option of running your vehicle as a 2x4 or a 4x4, usually by pushing a button on your dashboard or by using a shifter to select the mode you want. The majority of 4WD vehicles give you this option, and it is the best choice for most off-roading situations because you select the mode that is best for whatever road conditions you might face. Here's one thing to keep in mind with part-time 4WD systems, however: depending on your vehicle, you may or may not be able to switch between 2x4 and 4x4 operation "on the fly," that is, as you're driving. Be sure to check your owner's manual before you shift, not after!

- Automatic 4WD: This is the same as part-time 4WD except your vehicle decides when to run as a 2x4 and when to run as a 4x4—not you.

- Full-time 4WD: Full-time 4WD—also known as all-wheel drive (AWD) or permanent 4WD—means that your vehicle is designed to always run as a 4x4 and there's nothing you can do to make it run as a 2x4, this side of disconnecting a drive shaft. Relatively few 4WD vehicles are full-time 4WD, with the notable exception of Subaru, which has made the decision to produce only AWD vehicles.

Okay, so far so good. Now that you know a bit more about 4x4s, it's time to take a look at some of the

different 4x4 options you've got to choose from. If you look closely at your shifter or at the 4WD buttons or indicators on your console, you'll probably notice that you've got two 4WD options: 4H and 4L.

- 4H: 4H means 4x4 high range, which indicates that you are using the same gear ratios as you normally do for regular, on-road driving. This allows your vehicle to motor

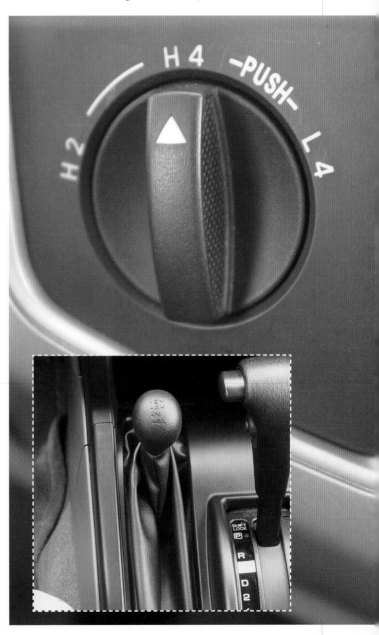

>> Transfer case levers and switches come in all kinds of shapes and sizes—and locations in your vehicle. Make sure you know where your switches are before you get off-road. *Ken Brubaker*

along at full speed (check your manual to see if your manufacturer suggests a maximum top speed while in 4H—some do). However, 4H limits your ability to do any serious crawling through the most common off-road obstacles such as mud, rocks, and steep hills, which require more torque (turning power) and less speed.

- 4L: 4L means 4x4 low range, which indicates that you are using special lower gear ratios that make your vehicle go much slower than normal, but that provide far more torque to your wheels. Selecting 4L allows you to tackle those off-road obstacles such as going up and down steep hills, working your way through serious mud, and doing all of those other extreme things you see in off-road magazines and websites. Remember, however, that 4L is generally limited to a top speed of about 25 miles per hour, and going faster than that may do bad things to your engine and drivetrain. Again, be sure to check your owner's manual before you make the shift.

By the way, you don't necessarily need to have a 4x4 to have fun off-roading. You might not know this, but almost every vehicle I've used for off-road racing—everything from the old Baja bugs I raced when I first started out, to the high-performance race trucks that we use for my Baja Protruck Racing Organization—has been two-wheel drive, not four-wheel drive. When you're going fast on an off-road race course, you don't want to be carrying around all the extra weight of an additional drive unit, and the extra parts are just something else to break. It's really only at the extremes—extreme silt, extreme hills, extreme mud, extreme snow—that you'll absolutely need four-wheel-drive.

But this book isn't about off-road racing, it's about off-road adventure. And for most off-road adventures, I recommend you bring along a four-wheel drive vehicle. You'll be more confident and more capable of dealing with the many different kinds of obstacles that you may

>> **An off-road vehicle can easily carry all that you need for a camping weekend. A pop-up trailer works well, but bear in mind that you'll want to leave the trailer behind you before you hit rough trail. That works well in places like this primitive camp site near Moab, Utah.** *Lee Klancher*

encounter along the way, and, when things really get hairy, you'll be glad you've got those extra two wheels pulling for you.

We've just about worked our way through the basics of what you need to know about how 4x4s work, but there's one more thing that you're likely to run across (especially if your vehicle is designed with serious off-roading in mind, such as Toyota's FJ Cruiser, the Hummer, or the ever-popular Jeep Wrangler): locking differentials. A differential (serious off-roaders call it a "pumpkin") is a round metal housing containing a set of gears between your drive shaft and your wheels, which, for most vehicles, allows one wheel on an axle to turn faster than the other through a turn—preventing wheel hop and making for a smoother ride.

There are three main kinds of differentials:

- Open: This is the standard differential that you'll find on most cars and trucks—even 4WD vehicles. While an open differential allows for smooth turns, the torque from your driveline will always seek the path of least resistance. So, if you've got one wheel on an axle up in the air, it will be spinning like mad while the one on the ground is sitting there doing nothing. Long story short, this does not make for a very effective off-roading scenario.

- Limited-slip: A limited-slip differential works like an open differential—up to a point. When either side-to-side torque difference or wheel speed exceeds a

>> **Just like transfer case levers and switches, the lever or switch to engage a locking differential might not be in the most obvious place. Know where it is and how to work it—before you need it!** *Ken Brubaker*

>> **Do you know where your differential is?**
Rick Shandley

certain point, the differential mechanically locks the two wheel shafts together, sending equal amounts of power to both wheels. You'll find limited-slip differentials most commonly used in race cars where they allow the vehicles to corner normally but kick in when one driving wheel gets unweighted in a hard turn and begins to overspin. They're also used in some 4WD vehicles.

- Locking: Most serious 4WD vehicles have locking differentials, often simply called lockers. A locking differential is essentially an open differential that allows you to lock the wheel shafts together. You can do this manually by activating a switch, or automatically, sending equal power to both wheels on an axle whether or not they are in contact with the ground.

This assures that every wheel is working to move you in whatever direction you decide to go.

A good friend of mine—Ron Stacey—was racing a two-wheel drive dune buggy in Baja when he got high centered on a bush with one rear wheel touching the ground and the other one up in the air. He didn't have a locking differential, so the tire up in the air spun when he pushed the accelerator, and the tire on the ground did nothing. He was stuck but good, there was no one around to tow him off the bush, and the clock was ticking. He thought about it for a while, and after tugging and pulling and jamming his finger he came up with what turned out to be a great way to get the effect of having a locking differential without actually installing one. He took a screwdriver and tightened the brake shoe on the wheel that was

>> **One of the great off-road destinations is Coco's Corner. Coco runs a little business near Puertocitos. He started it years ago to provide service to stranded Baja racers, and still offers repair service, cold drinks, and great stories told to anyone who stops in.** *Lee Klancher*

CHAPTER 1: GET READY FOR TRAVEL ADVENTURE

up in the air. That made the tire on the ground start moving, and he was able to get off the bush and back into the race. You'd be amazed what kind of ideas you can come up with when you step back for a minute and set your mind to it.

There are some other terms that you should take some time to get familiar with—phrases such as ground clearance, breakover angle, angle of approach, and more—but I'll save these items for the section later in this chapter titled Knowing Your Limits (and Staying Within Them).

PICKING A DESTINATION

When you're thinking about going off road, picking a destination and making plans can be almost as much fun as actually making the trip. Notice that I said almost. So, how do you find the ultimate off-road travel adventure? Here are a few steps that will help you find the perfect place for you:

1. What's the primary goal of your trip? Do you want to do some great fishing, explore a historical area such as abandoned Colorado mining towns, or camp on the beach? Narrow your choices down to ones that fulfill the primary goal of your trip and discard the rest—at least until your next off-road adventure!

2. Seek recommendations. If you're looking for the ultimate adventure travel destination, then who better to ask than someone who has already done it? Ask around, visit websites where other adventure travelers hang out or leave trip reports, watch extreme travel shows on TV, and read off-road and

>> **When you are traveling off road, you'll often find yourself in old mining districts. Stopping to see an old mine or ghost town can be a great way to spend a day off road.** *Lee Klancher*

travel magazines and articles in the travel section of your local newspaper.

3. Check 'em out. When you've narrowed your short list down to a few recommendations, thoroughly check out each of your candidates. Get as much information as you can and then make a decision based on what you think will work best for you. Okay—now you're all set!

Keep in mind that the destination you choose will impact your off-road adventure in many ways—ways that you'll need to consider as you prepare for your journey. Think about how your answers to the following questions will affect the preparations you make for your trip:

- What's the climate going to be like—blazing hot desert, freezing cold mountains, or something in between?

- Is your adventure going to take place over a long weekend, or do you plan to unplug from your regular life for an entire week or maybe even a month?

- Will you be towing a trailer or boat?

- Will the off-road trails you'll be driving be technically challenging or pretty tame?

- Do you know the difficulty of the trails you will encounter, and are you experienced enough to drive them?

- Will you be traveling to your destination as a caravan, with a group of other off-roaders, or will you be going it alone?

- Will you need special government permits or permission of private property owners to drive in certain areas?

- Will you need to make reservations weeks or months in advance?

- Will you need to bring along passports or obtain visas or special insurance before you cross the border?

- Will you be camping at your destination or settling into an RV park, cabin, or motel?

- Will you need to carry extra gas?

- Will you need to carry food?

- Will you need to carry cooking and camping equipment?

- What kind of maps and/or navigation equipment will you need?

The answers to these questions—and many others like them—will have a definite impact on what you'll need to do to prepare for your off-road adventure. Take time to ask yourself questions like the ones listed here—based on your particular destination—and be sure you prepare accordingly before you hit the road.

KNOWING YOUR LIMITS (AND STAYING WITHIN THEM)

If there's one thing I tell people over and over, it's this: Don't make mistakes.

So, how do you avoid making mistakes? First, get the right vehicle for the job you've got in mind. You wouldn't drive an old Buick station wagon on the Rubicon Trail, would you? That would definitely be a big mistake. Second, know the limits of your vehicle, and stay within them.

If you pay close attention—and you should pay close attention—your vehicle will tell you when you're driving outside of its limits and when you are driving beyond your own skills. If you're going so fast that you're sliding off the road, then your vehicle is sending you a message loud and clear—you're operating your vehicle outside of its limits. The solution? Slow down and get within the limits of your vehicle.

When you're driving off road, just a couple of inches can make the difference between falling off a cliff, hitting a tree, or hitting a sharp rock that's going to give you a flat tire, so you've got to know exactly where your tires are—not just sometimes, but all the time. When I was driving a $500,000 Toyota Trophy race truck, I had to know exactly where that vehicle was, no matter how fast I was driving—and I was driving fast! It's the same

>> Some off-road adventures will make your rig think it's turned into a pretzel. Your job is to make sure you don't make that pretzel permanent as you navigate a particularly challenging obstacle. *Ken Brubaker*

thing when you're driving on a regular highway. If you drift across the double-yellow line and into oncoming traffic, you're going to have a problem. That's a mistake. If you get lost in a race, that's a mistake. If you get stuck in the mud, that's a mistake.

And your job is to avoid making mistakes.

Staying within your limits—and the limits of your vehicle—requires knowing some additional lingo:

- Trail ratings: Many off-road trails have been given a numerical rating or score, which represents how difficult they are to drive. There are a few different rating systems in place. On the East Coast of the U.S., off-roaders tend to use a 10-point scale, with 1 being easiest and 10 being most difficult. Only vehicles that have been highly modified to handle extreme obstacles will be able to negotiate trails with the highest ratings. On the West Coast, off-roaders seem to prefer a 4-point scale, with 1 again being easiest and 4 being most difficult. You might also find a rating system in use that's similar to the one used to rate ski runs where a green trail is easy, a blue trail is of intermediate difficulty, and a black trail is most difficult. You might even see a double black diamond— the most difficult trail of them all.

- Ground clearance: If you do much off-road driving, you've probably encountered a rock or two big enough for you to wonder whether or not you'd be able to make it over without scraping the bottom of your vehicle, or sometimes worse—high bottoming. This happens when your chassis gets pushed up on a rock or

>> **When approaching a hill or other obstacle, it's always a good idea to know if you've got a sufficient angle of approach to climb it without leaving your bumper (or worse!) behind.** *Rick Shandley*

CHAPTER 1: GET READY FOR TRAVEL ADVENTURE

large bump, and one or more of your tires loses its contact with the ground, leaving you stuck. Your vehicle's ground clearance—the distance between the ground and the lowest hanging portion of your vehicle's undercarriage—is what determines whether you'll make it over an obstacle or not. Most off-road vehicles are designed to maximize ground clearance, but even so, you need to be aware of how much clearance you've got and keep an eye on the height of obstacles you encounter along the way. Here's a tip: Whenever possible, drive your tire directly over the obstacle—as slowly as possible—rather than straddling it. This will help ensure that you won't get hung up.

- Angle of approach: The angle of approach, or approach angle, is the steepest angle you can approach and drive up an obstacle or incline without scraping the front bumper or other lower components located in the front of your vehicle. While a stock Chevy TrailBlazer has an approach angle of about 29 degrees, a Hummer H1 runs a whopping 72 degrees! The bigger the number, the steeper the hill or obstacle you'll be able to drive up without dragging your front end or getting it stuck.

- Angle of departure: The angle of departure, or departure angle, is the steepest angle you can descend off a

>> **Watch your angle of approach when crossing ditches and gulleys—not just when approaching the bottom of a hill.** *Rick Shandley*

hill or other obstacle without striking the rear bumper or other lower components at the rear of your vehicle. At 37.5 degrees, the Hummer H1 beats the pants off of most other factory SUVs, such as the Ford Explorer at 24 degrees. Like the angle of approach, the bigger the number, the steeper the hill you'll be able to tackle without getting hung up.

- Breakover angle: Breakover angle is similar to approach angle and departure angle, but applies to the middle of your vehicle. It is the sharpest angle a vehicle can straddle without hitting the underside. For example, if you crest a small hill or drive over a large boulder, the breakover angle will determine whether or not the middle of your chassis will get hung up on it. Stock SUVs have an average breakover angle of 20 degrees, while a Hummer H1 runs 35 degrees. Again, a bigger number is better.

Keep in mind that all of these different angles and clearances can change if you make certain modifications to your vehicle. For example, if you go to a taller tire and wheel package, you're going to raise the overall height of your vehicle, which will increase your available ground clearance and result in a higher breakover angle. A suspension lift will also give you more ground clearance and increase your breakover angle. A body lift is unlikely to give you any additional ground clearance because your differential, oil pan, and other parts will still be hanging in the same place, ready to get nailed by a rock, but you will probably end up with better angles of approach and departure because your

>> opposite and above: **Be sure you have some idea of what your breakover angle is before you decide to cross over an obstacle—not after you get stuck!** *Rick Shandley*

CHAPTER 1: GET READY FOR TRAVEL ADVENTURE

PREVIOUS PAGE \ LEFT >> **This is what off-road travel adventure is all about—new places, new people, and new perspectives on this great land in which we live.** *Ken Brubaker*

front and rear bumpers and fascia will be higher off the ground.

Staying within the limits of my vehicles and within my own limits as a driver have many times meant the difference between winning and losing races. Invariably, when I lost a race I should have won, it was because I stepped outside of those limits—sometimes only for a second or two—but it only takes an instant to make a mistake that can ruin your entire day.

This is important, so I'll say it again: Know the limits of your vehicle, and know your own limits as a driver. If you're driving a Hummer, your limits are going to be much higher than if you're driving a Volkswagen Beetle. If you've got years of off-road driving experience, your limits will also be much higher than if you've never driven off road in your life. As you get more familiar with driving off road and more comfortable with your rig, you'll improve your skills and gain the confidence that will turn you into a seasoned off-roader before you know it.

READY, SET, GO!

In the chapters that follow, you'll find everything you need to know about preparing for your off-road travel adventure, including what to bring, what to drive, rules of the road, what to do before leaving, helping others, and respecting the environment. While driving is definitely one of the most enjoyable parts of any off-road travel adventure, remember that there's plenty else to enjoy as well. Going to new places, seeing new things, meeting new people, enjoying quality time with friends and family, encountering new challenges—and conquering them—all are important elements of the off-road experience.

Take your time, have fun, and enjoy the ride!

... IT PAYS TO TAKE A MINUTE OR TWO TO THINK ABOUT

chapter 2

>>WHAT TO BRING

Before you go anywhere—whether on or off road—it pays to take a minute or two to think about what conditions or situations you might encounter, and the best things to bring along so you're prepared in case something bad happens. For example, who would have thought that carrying a pair of blankets in your vehicle is a must for off-road adventuring in the hot desert? It's true. If you get stuck in the sand, a blanket laid out in front of each stuck wheel will give you the traction you're missing and help get you on your way. Who would imagine that a mobile phone would have a rat's chance of working out in the middle of nowhere? As it turns out, cellular phone towers are rapidly appearing in even the most remote areas—much to the consternation of those who would prefer to

031

PREVIOUS PAGE >> **It's almost always more fun (and safer) to share your off-road adventures with friends and family.** *Ken Brubaker*

look at soaring trees than at a big, steel antenna—making access to help more easily available when you need it the most. The coverage is not yet complete, so you'll still need a satellite phone in most remote areas, but it's getting better. Also, don't forget your insurance, GPS, and first-aid kit.

Of course, there's more to ensuring that your off-road adventure is going to be a safe one than simply bringing along a box of whatever you might need in case something bad happens along the way. It's far better to prevent something bad from happening by making sure that you've got the right vehicle for the job, that it's in good repair, and that it's gassed up and ready to go. As the old saying goes, an ounce of prevention can be worth a pound of cure.

THINK ABOUT YOUR GOALS

What are the goals for your off-road adventure? Are you looking forward to finding some peace and quiet—away from the hustle and bustle of your everyday life—in a remote corner of your county or state? Do you want to see if those mud and snow tires you bought last week are up to snuff? Are you planning to join a group of friends going to explore an old ghost town out in the desert? Or do you just want to get some fresh air and sunshine down at the beach?

>> **My trusty Baja bag—I never leave home without it!** *Rick Shandley*

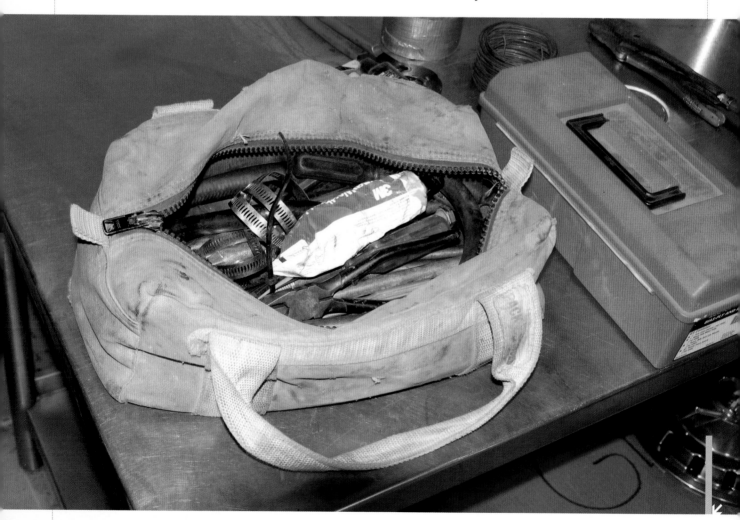

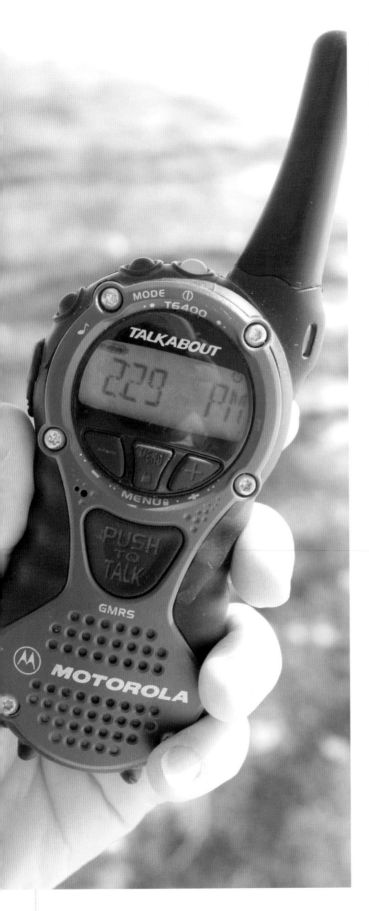

I have found it helpful before starting any adventure—whether on road or off road—to set some goals for the trip. Setting goals helps give you direction, and it helps ensure that your off-road adventure will be the kind of experience you hoped it would be. Your own goals will usually quickly become apparent when you ask questions like:

- Do I need to be someplace by a certain date or time?

- Is the adventure going to be an informal one where it really doesn't matter where I end up, or is it going to be a formally planned one with a specific destination in mind?

- Do I need to make plans for overnight sleeping arrangements?

- Am I going on my adventure to see something new, or am I going to a familiar place?

- Do I want to learn some new skills, or practice some old ones?

Throughout my life, I've always been a goal setter, and I understand the power of turning a lot of little goals into big goals. My long-term goal was never to be an off-road race car driver. From the time I was in the third grade, I knew exactly what I wanted to be when I grew up: the general superintendent of the Atlas Fence Company in San Diego, California. Racing was something I did during my time off just for fun because my system needed it. For as long as I can remember, I have been racing or competing in something, and my attention-deficit-disorder body just needed that racing.

Setting career goals and then making steady progress toward them taught me how to set and reach my goals in racing. I worked for a lot of different companies. I was a laborer, then a labor foreman, and then an ironworker for a long time. But, guess what? When I turned 30, I reached my big

>> **When you're traveling with a buddy, a pair of FM radios just might be your best friend.** *Ken Brubaker*

goal in life: I got that job as general superintendent of the Atlas Fence Company. Life was good, but it didn't take long—about two years—until I started to wish I had set a bigger goal! But I learned a lot from reaching that first big goal, and it made a huge difference in my next 30 years as I started winning races and turning off-road racing into a full-time profession—and life.

ANTICIPATE BEFORE YOU PARTICIPATE

So, you're getting ready to go on your off-road adventure. As you get prepared, ask yourself some questions: Where are you going—to a popular off-roading area close to home, or far away? Are you going in the middle of the week or on the weekend? If you go in the middle of the week there won't be as many people around because most off-roaders do their thing on weekends and holidays. So, if you get hurt or something bad happens to your rig on a weekday, it's going to be a lot harder to get help. Right off the bat, I recommend bringing someone else—and another vehicle—with you so you can help each other out. Find a friend you get along with. I have a friend who loves to go to the gym with a buddy of his because he has got so much more experience, and my friend learns a lot every time he goes to the gym with his buddy.

There's a whole list of items that I recommend you bring along with you, which I have detailed in the next section of this chapter. If you're going to a desolate spot, where other adventurers will be few and far between, let people know where you're going and when you'll be back.

>> **Practice letting air out of your tires before you get off road.** *Rick Shandley*

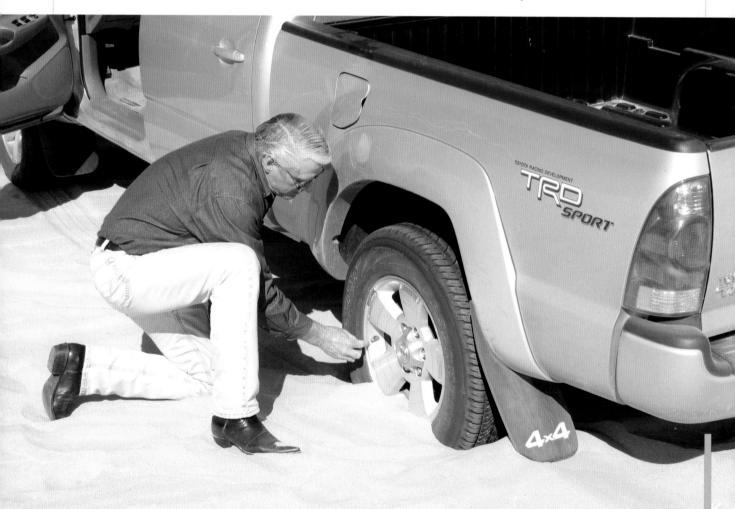

In addition, a tow strap is one of the most important things you can bring with you, along with a first-aid kit and a fire extinguisher. Put everything into a box that's secure in your car and not bouncing around. Find a net that you can throw over the box or tie it down. I like to use those hard plastic milk carton boxes. You can easily fit a fire extinguisher, a tow strap, a little shovel, and a first-aid kit in one of those.

I also recommend bringing a Baja bag, which I use to carry my set of essential tools. I like to carry a good pair of Channellocks because I'm not going to carry a great big box of tools when I need an 11/16-inch socket and a 1/2-inch-drive ratchet. Look around your car and make sure you have a jack that works. I can't even count how many times I've seen a guy blow a tire and then find out that his jack is gone or does-

n't work, and that his spare tire doesn't have air in it. As mentioned earlier, cell phones often work out in the sticks, so don't leave yours at home. I also like to have radio communication on board—either a CB or FM radio. We mostly use FM radios, which work much better than the somewhat-dated CB radios.

Being mentally prepared is perhaps the most important thing you can do before you go on your off-road adventure. Take time to give some real thought to where you are going to go and what you expect to encounter. Let's say you're going way out in the desert during the middle of the week in August, and there are not going to be too many people where you're going. Knowing that temperatures will be well over 100 degrees for much of the day, water's going to be very high on your list of things to bring.

>> **When you're in the deep sand, having a low tire pressure works best.** *Rick Shandley*

If you do make a mistake and get stuck (don't worry about it, we all make mistakes from time to time), think about how you are going to tell someone where you are because when you're out in the middle of the desert there's not going to be a sign that says you're at the corner of 33rd Street and Maple View. You'll need a topographical map and a GPS with you. If you have a breakdown, those two tools will tell you exactly where you are so that when you get in touch with rescuers—via cell or satellite phone or by any other method—you can tell them how to find you.

I'm not saying this to scare you away from going off-roading. I want you to go off road and have a great time. There are some great things to do and some remarkable places to see in this great big country of ours—and next door in Canada and Mexico for that matter—but I want to make sure you think about what you are doing instead of just going out there by yourself in a vehicle that doesn't have a spare tire with air.

Speaking of air, before you take your vehicle into any serious off-road adventures, be sure to practice letting your tire pressure down. One thing that's typically going to happen in off-roading, even with a four-wheel-drive vehicle, is that you are going to get stuck on level ground. This predicament occurs because if you've got 40 pounds of air pressure in your tires, the tires are not going to hook up very well. With a lower tire pressure, the tread can flex and grip the ground.

If you've got a low-pressure tire gauge, as soon

>> **It pays to invest in a low-pressure tire gauge—regular gauges aren't calibrated to the pressures you'll need when you're adventuring off road.** *Rick Shandley*

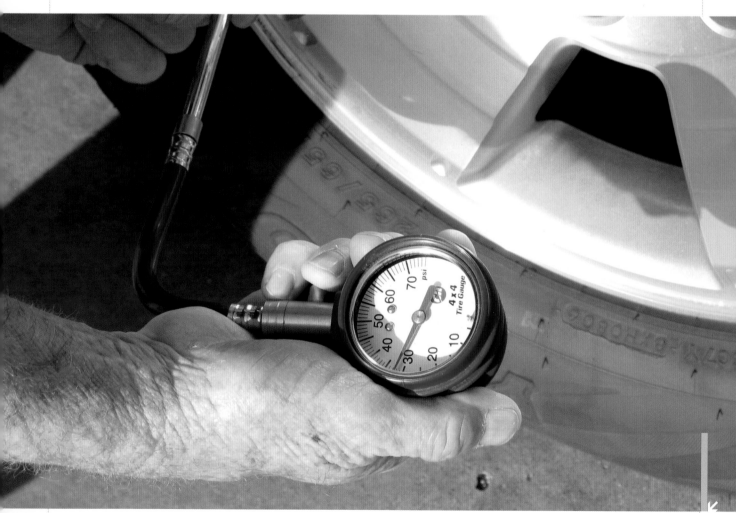

as your tires start to slip, you can stop and let the tire pressure down to about 8 pounds, kick the dirt away from the front of the tires, and get going again. Once you get through the tough stuff, then you simply inflate your tires again and get on your way. You did bring a compressor or air pump with you, right? If you don't have an air pump, you can drive down the highway—slowly—to a gas station to fill up your tires and then go on your merry way.

TOP 10 LIST OF THINGS TO BRING

While there are plenty of off-road destinations close to civilization, others are out of the way. For example, if your idea of off-road fun is running the power line roads a couple of miles from home, you can probably walk right out and find help easily and quickly if your rig breaks down. If you're somewhere up in the Ozarks exploring old mining ruins in the middle of nowhere and have a breakdown, you've got a problem—all the more reason to be prepared.

So, while my top 10 list of things to bring for your off-road adventure includes the basics to help in most any situation, you should customize this list and make your own depending on where you're going. For example, you probably won't need a heavy, goose-down-filled coat in the middle of summer no matter where you're going, but a few jugs of water are essential whether you're hundreds of miles away from home or just down the road. Before you go, take a few minutes to think ahead

>> **Be sure to have a first-aid kit with you. You might never need it, but you'll be glad you've got it in the event that you—or someone else—does.** *Ken Brubaker*

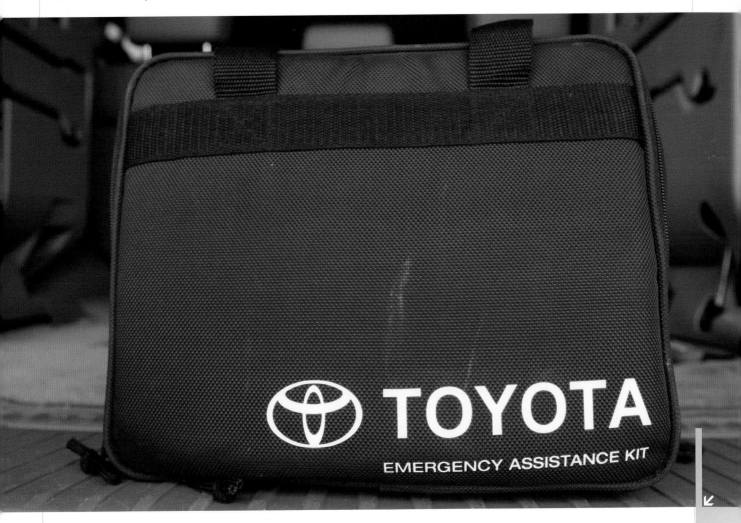

to what kinds of conditions you might encounter, and be prepared!

HERE'S MY TOP 10 LIST:

1. Water. For you, your friends, your kids, your pets, and your vehicle. And, no, beer is not a recommended replacement for water in your radiator. The general rule of thumb is to bring at least one gallon of water per person per day. Figure another couple of gallons for your vehicle in case it decides to boil over. Just don't go too crazy because water is heavy, and it takes up a lot of space in your vehicle.

2. Low-pressure tire gauge. An air pressure gauge is one of the most important things to bring along with you on any off-road adventure, but not just any old air pressure gauge will do. To be of any use for off-roading, it's got to be a low-pressure gauge. Why? Because letting air out of your tires is one of the best ways to get through sand and a variety of other tough off-road obstacles. If the gauge starts at 30 pounds, it won't do you any good. It's got to go down to 7 or 8 pounds.

3. First-aid kit. You'll need more than just one of those cheapo ones with just a Band-Aid or two and a set of rusty tweezers. Splurge on a decent kit with a good selection of basic items to deal

>> *right:* **GPS systems come in several different flavors—some are handheld and portable, while others may be permanently built into your vehicle.** *left:* **Ideally, the GPS system you choose should be able to display maps of the areas in which you plan to travel.** *Ken Brubaker*

with a variety of first-aid needs. You're not going to need to do surgery out there, but be sure you can deal with a couple of major cuts and abrasions. A snake bite kit is also a good addition.

4. Tow strap or winch. If you're adventuring off road, there's a good chance you will get stuck at least once or twice, especially if you like your adventure in the extreme. So, bring along a tow strap (also known as a recovery strap) or winch, which will soon be your best friend. Notice I said tow strap! Don't even think about bringing along a tow chain instead of a strap. Chains are dangerous, and many seasoned off-roaders will refuse to hook up to you if that's all you've got. On the other hand, the other driver may have their own tow strap to help if you need it. Be sure to check out the Tips For Getting Unstuck sidebar on page 44 for more information on the proper use of these essential off-roading tools.

5. Mobile or satellite phone. A phone is the best way to get help if you're off road and need help—or if you want someone to deliver a pizza to you and your co-adventurers. Some vehicles today—such as Acura, Subaru, and General Motors cars and trucks with the OnStar communications system—come with their own phones built in, so you'll always have one with you no matter where you go. Bear in mind that, as mentioned previously, mobile phones sometimes have no service in remote areas. If you are headed deep into the wilderness, don't count on a mobile phone as your only fallback plan. If

>> **A basic set of tools is a definite must for any off-road adventure.** *Rick Shandley*

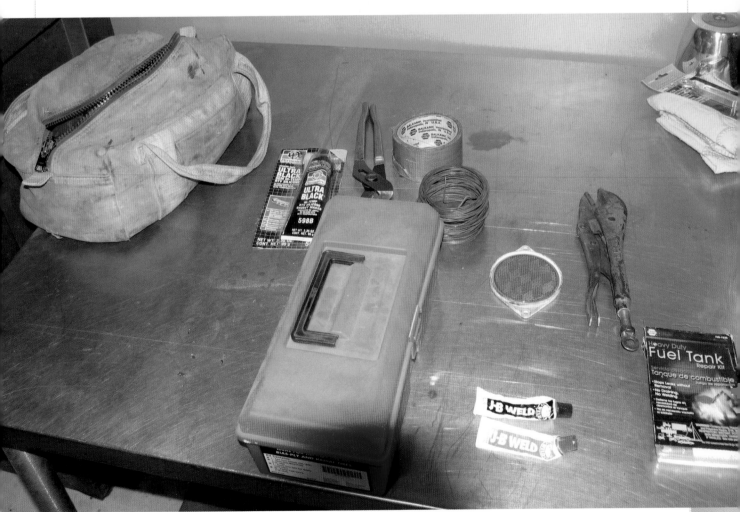

you are going for an extended trip in the back-country, consider renting a satellite phone.

6. Global positioning system. Better known simply as GPS, this is exactly what you'll need to find your way back to a road, or even back to civilization, when you get a bit too far off the beaten track. While many vehicles today come with a built in GPS/navigation unit, you can save money by purchasing a quality portable unit that can be shared by all your vehicles.

7. Flashlight. Even if you are just planning a day trip, if you get stuck out in the middle of nowhere, your day trip may soon turn into a night trip and you'll need a flashlight. Flashlights also come in handy in the middle of the day if you need a good look at something deep in your engine compartment or under-neath your rig. Keep one in your glove compart-ment at all times, and make sure the batteries are fresh. Better yet, pick up a wind-up flashlight that gets rid of the need for batteries altogether by generating its own electricity.

8. Set of basic tools. I'm not suggesting you bring a big, heavy tool box with every single Craftsman socket ever made—in metric, SAE,

>> **If you're planning to go on a serious, highly technical off-road adventure, invest in detailed topo-graphic maps that will give you a more precise picture of the terrain, along with milestones and poten-tial hazards. While computer-based topographic maps are very powerful tools, paper maps are the old standby—and they don't need batteries.** *Ken Brubaker*

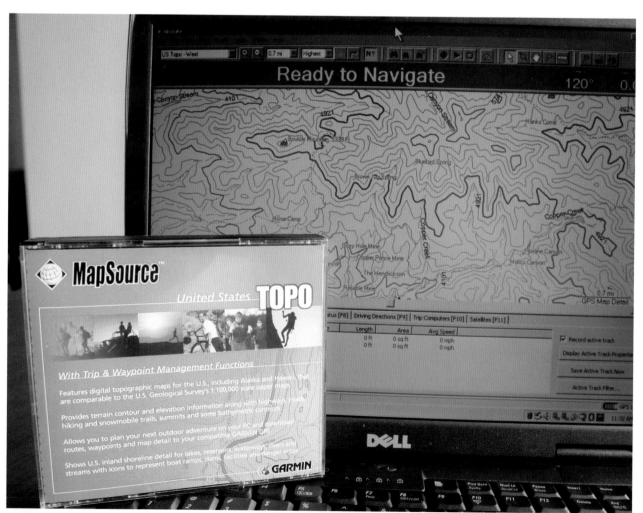

and English sizes. But you should have a basic selection of wrenches, screwdrivers, pliers, and other tools that you can keep in a bag in your trunk or luggage area. I keep mine in a Baja bag.

9. Battery jumper cables. If your battery conks out and you need a boost to get your engine restarted, you'll be very happy that you brought a set of jumper cables. Don't assume another driver will have a set. Bring your own, and be sure to get some nice, long ones because if you're stuck in a position that's hard to get to, you'll need the extra slack.

10. A buddy. It's always a good idea—and more fun—to enjoy your off-road adventures with a buddy in another vehicle. If your vehicle breaks down or gets stuck, you'll have your friend in the other vehicle to help tow you out, give you a jump start, or run and get help. I highly recommend including your friends and family in your off-road adventures. For me, a group of two or three is just right. There are some people who love to go out in larger groups—five or six or more—and there's nothing wrong with that, but I personally like a smaller group that won't get bogged down by someone who doesn't know what they are doing. I've taken big groups to Mexico and had a great time with them as long as I controlled the situation. It's true that there is safety in numbers.

Okay, that's my top 10 list of things to bring for off-road adventures. Additionally, be sure to

>> **Got a winch? Bring it!**

engage your brain, and take some time to think about exactly where you're going, what kind of conditions you're likely to encounter, and what situations you might need to get into or out of as safely as possible. In that spirit, here's a list of other items you might want to consider bringing, depending on your particular situation. Again, try to keep your list down to the essentials. You don't want to have to haul a trailer or leave your passengers behind just to bring everything you might possibly need along with you.

- Spare-in-a-can
- Compact air compressor
- Fire extinguisher

- Food
- CB or FM two-way radio or walkie-talkies
- Camera
- Sunglasses
- Sunscreen
- Matches
- Plastic trash bags
- Maps
- Insect repellant
- Hat
- Leather work gloves
- Rags
- Blanket
- Shovel
- Oil and other vehicle fluids

>> **It pays to plan. Lay out your planned route before you start your off-road adventure, and estimate when and where you'll make any refueling stops and overnight stays. Give a copy to a friend or relative before you leave in case you get stuck and are unable to get help.** *Ken Brubaker*

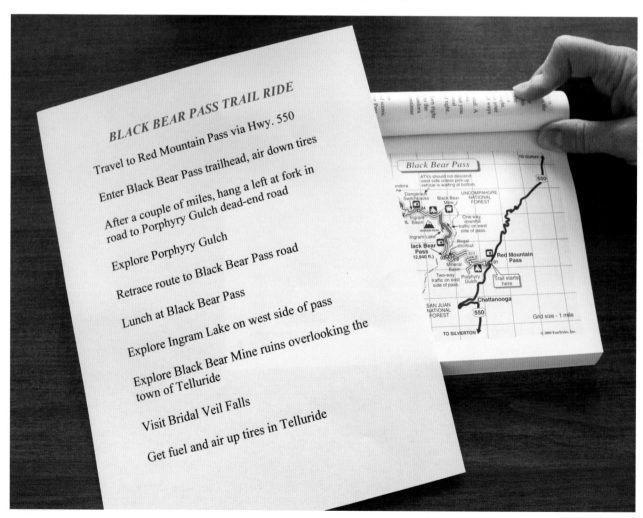

>>TOOLS OF THE TRADE<<

Whether you're a master mechanic or your idea of auto repair is dropping your car off at a local shop, it's important to bring at least a set of basic tools along on your off-road adventures. Use the following checklist when you put your own set of tools together. In the case of combination and socket wrenches, bring along an assortment of standard and metric—nowadays, many vehicles use a mix of both.

- Screwdrivers (standard & Phillips—small, medium, and large)
- Pliers (needle nose, Channellocks, Vise-Grip)
- Wrenches (Allen, crescent, open-end combination box)
- Standard and deep socket wrenches (3/8- and 1/2-inch drive)
- Torx sockets
- Pry bar
- Jackknife
- Hammer
- Duct tape

- Wood blocks
- Equipment tie downs
- Toilet paper or paper towels
- Compass
- Additional fuel cans with fuel

You never know when you might need something, or when what you've left behind might come in handy. One time when Parnelli Jones was racing in Baja, a bug flew in his ear and there was no way that it was going to come back out on its own. I guess it kind of liked its new home. Parnelli decided that using a screwdriver to fish it out might not be the best thing to do. So what did he decide to do? He figured out he could use a light to attract the bug and get it to crawl out on its own. But he didn't have a flashlight strong enough to do the job. Now what was he supposed to do? Parnelli found a farmer who had a generator at his house. They started the generator, and held a light bulb up to Parnelli's ear. The bug saw the light and wandered out.

THE $64,000 FOUR-WHEEL DRIVE QUESTION

Here's a question that I'm often asked: Do I really need four-wheel drive for my off-road adventure? The simple answer is: It depends.

For a surprisingly wide variety of off-road situations, you probably don't need four-wheel drive. If your vehicle has enough clearance, you'll be able to get by just fine with two-wheel drive. As I mentioned

>> **You don't necessarily need four-wheel drive to have fun off road; two-wheel drive will often suffice.**
Ken Brubaker

>>TIPS FOR GETTING UNSTUCK<<

Regardless of how thoroughly you plan and how carefully you drive, chances are you're going to eventually get stuck or get in a position where you can't move. If that's the case, then you'll be glad that you brought two things with you: (1) a tow strap, and (2) a buddy in another vehicle to pull you out. But the solution is not quite as simple as just tying a rope to your bumper. You've got to have the right equipment, and you've got to use it the right way.

>> **When you really get stuck (and it does happen from time to time), a hi-lift jack might be just what the doctor ordered.** *Ken Brubaker*

- Use a nylon tow strap rated at least to 10,000 pounds. No chains or metal hooks. If they snap, they can do tremendous damage to life, limb, windows, and body panels.

- Damage often occurs when the tow strap is hooked up incorrectly. If either vehicle isn't equipped with a tow hook, the strap should be placed around the spring shackles or frame in the front. (Bumpers tear off extremely easily.) Then, tow in the direction of least resistance.

- Place a heavy rag or floor mat over the center of the tightened tow strap. Should the strap snap, this can help keep the ends from flying up and hurting you or the vehicles.

- If high-centered, you can often jack up the side with the least amount of traction and build a surface using rocks, wood, branches, or even your floor mats.

- A Hi-Lift-style or appropriate jack is very versatile because of its design, and it may be the only jack that will get your rig high enough off the ground to make a difference. Make sure there is a proper place for the jack to fit snugly on the vehicle.

- Mud or deep sand can cause problems for a jack. Using a block of wood or even your floor mat under the jack's base can keep the jack from sinking further into the sand or mud.

Be sure to read the instructions that come with your tow strap. It's important to take good care of the strap so it will be ready when you need it. Do not use a strap that is damaged, frayed, or cut. Store your strap out of sunlight because the ultraviolet rays can damage the nylon and make it weak. Also, keep it away from heat and dirt. Particles of dirt and mud can work their way into your strap and cut away at the strands over a period of time, weakening it. So, after every use, be sure to clean off your strap with a good spray of water, and then dry it off before you put it away for the next time you need it.

before, most of my off-road racing—including the Baja 500 and Baja 1000—was done in highly modified two-wheel drive vehicles. When you are on an off-road adventure, however, a four-wheel-drive vehicle can give you some extra peace of mind.

The real usefulness of four-wheel drive becomes apparent whenever you get into the extremes—extreme hill climbing, extreme silt, extreme snow, extreme sand, or extreme rocks or mud. People drive in snow all the time with two-wheel drive and they do just fine, but it's definitely better to have four-wheel drive. You can get across sand easily in two-wheel drive just by decreasing your tire pressure—especially if you've got a locking rear-end of some sort, and off-road tires with better flotation—but again, four-wheel drive works better.

So the final answer to this $64,000 question depends on where you're going, what kind of terrain you expect to encounter, and your personal level of off-road driving experience. Personally, for a typical recreational off-roading experience, I would take a four-wheel drive vehicle, and I would be sure I wasn't in a hurry. Going too fast is one thing that's bound to get you into trouble. I've made most of my off-roading mistakes because I got in too much of a hurry and I didn't think far enough ahead. As a professional racer, it was my job to go fast. When you are on the trail for fun, bear in mind that being in a hurry to get home for the big game, a doctor appointment, or any of the other daily issues of modern life is not a good enough reason to rush. There's a big difference between going fast in a race and getting careless in the backcountry.

>> **Before embarking on any off-road adventure, be sure to create a pre-trip checklist—and then use it!**
Ken Brubaker

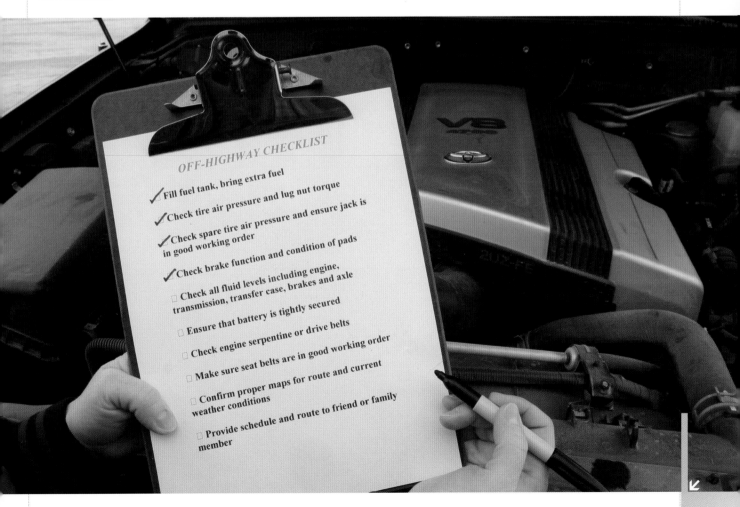

PRE-OFF-ROAD ADVENTURE CHECKLIST

You know how pilots go through a preflight checklist before they take off? They do that to make sure their airplane is ready to go, that everything works the way it's supposed to, and that they haven't forgotten something obvious—like putting gas in the fuel tanks—that might cause them to make an unscheduled stop along the way. Before you embark on your own off-road adventure, you should go through your own pre-off-road checklist. You'll be safer, you'll have peace of mind, and you'll have a lot more fun.

Before you go, be sure to:

- Check your tires—including your spare!—for damage and proper air pressure. Also check that your lug nuts aren't loose.

- Check to be sure that your jack is where it's supposed to be, that all the parts are there, and that it works.

- Check to see that your brakes are in good working order and that your brake fluid reservoir is topped up.

- Check all fluid levels.

- Be sure your battery is strapped down, particularly if you're going to be doing some serious bouncing around.

- Check your engine drive belts.

- Make sure your seat belts are working well and not frayed or damaged.

- Make sure you've got the right maps, and obtain any required permits.

- Let someone know your planned schedule and route.

- Check the weather conditions for your planned destination as well as along the route you will use to get there.

- Fill your gas tank.

Last but not least, a warning: Driving takes 100 percent of your concentration. If you've gone through the above checklists and equipped your vehicle appropriately for your off-road adventure, then the inside of your vehicle is now full of a lot of "stuff." Don't add to your distraction by allowing that stuff to get in your way, bounce around, and hit you in the head. Tie down loose objects in your vehicle so they can't roll around and cause you to lose your concentration or—perhaps most dangerously—end up under your pedals. That also means keeping the top of your dashboard clear of items that will cause distractions and reflect back in your windshield. Be prepared to drive! Focus and concentration make driving easier, safer, and more fun.

>> **Be sure to check your tire pressure before you start your trip—and after you lower your air pressure to cross sand or rocks. And don't forget to check your spare!** *Ken Brubaker*

>> **Where will your off-road adventure take you?** *Rick Shandley*

...THERE ARE A FEW RULES OF THE ROAD

DEPARTMEN OF THE INTERIOR
OF LAND MANAGEMENT

BUREAU OF LAND MANAGEMENT

BITTER SPRING TRAIL

National

Back Country Byway

chapter 3

>>THE OFF-ROAD ADVENTURER'S CODE<<

Before you get going on your adventure, there are a few rules of the road, or, more accurately, rules of the off road, which you'll need to know. This knowledge will help you drive like a seasoned veteran instead of a rookie. Plus, these rules will teach you to leave the places you visit just like you found them. I have put together my Off-Road Adventurer's Code for a variety of different reasons—some for safety, others for

PREVIOUS PAGE >> **Routes that are legal to travel by off-road vehicles are usually clearly marked. Take the time to make yourself aware of local regulations.** *Lee Klancher*

etiquette, and yet others to minimize your impact on the fragile ecosystems and geologic formations that are often very much a part of many of the best off-roading areas.

Follow this Code—and the recommendations of the nonprofit organization Tread Lightly! (detailed later in this chapter)—and not only will you have a better off-roading experience, but so will the guy or gal who follows you.

HELPING OTHERS

There is a tremendous camaraderie among off-road racers. If someone has an accident or is seriously injured, you don't think twice. You simply stop and help. Now, you might wonder about this rule of stopping to help someone, especially if you're in a fiercely competitive race, with a lot of your time and money invested in your rig, your crew, your training, and your supplies set up along the way. You do it because you have to help. Out in the middle of nowhere, there may be no one else to help, and the racers depend on one another for their safety. Lives are at stake, and those who are stranded or injured in an accident are depending on you. The other side of the coin is that you may be depending on them for help the next time around.

>> **When it comes to getting a stuck vehicle moving again, having a friend (or two or three) along to help can make all the difference in the world. As the old saying goes, many hands make light work.** *Ken Brubaker*

IVAN "IRONMAN" STEWART'S OFF-ROAD ADVENTURER'S CODE

- Set goals. Know where you're going, how soon you want to get there, and what you hope to accomplish.

- Be prepared. Expect the unexpected—and the expected—and be prepared to deal with both.

- Bring your top mental game. Stay sharp and don't get too cocky or overconfident. That's when mistakes are most apt to happen.

- Don't make mistakes. Mistakes are a sure way to spoil even the best off-road adventure. My advice? Whenever possible, don't make them. We all make mistakes from time to time, but do try to keep them to a minimum.

- Stay within the boundaries. This applies to the boundaries of your journey (staying on marked trails, for example), the boundaries of your equipment (you're asking for trouble if you drive across a steep hill), and your own boundaries (driving faster than your experience will support).

- Don't be in a hurry. Take your time. Enjoy the scenery. Being in a hurry often leads to mistakes and can result in serious damage to your rig—and to you. Go as slowly as possible, but as fast as necessary.

- Respect your environment. Don't forget—there are a lot of other people who would like to enjoy the places you visit. Be sure to leave it in as good condition or better when you depart as it was when you arrived.

- Help others. If someone is in trouble and needs your help—and it's not going to risk your own life or limb—by all means help. You may be the only other person he or she sees all day—or all week.

- Bring a buddy. It's generally safer (and often more fun) to travel with another rig or two.

>> **Don't be in a hurry. Remember: Go as slowly as possible, but as fast as necessary.** *Rick Shandley*

This exact thing has happened to me many times. I've been in races where I encountered someone broken down along the way. I gave him some gas, or checked in my Baja bag—where I keep my tools and spare parts—and gave him a nut and bolt, or a fan belt, or whatever he might have needed. Sure enough, the next day I'm the one who's broken down on the side of the road, and that same guy I helped the day before helps me. That's why you've got to stop and help. In a racing situation, if the guy's not hurt, he might just wave you on.

Over the years, I've spent a lot of time off road—some of it racing, and some of it just having fun exploring with family and friends. One thing I've learned in all those years is that it's important to respect the outdoors and to treat it the way you would want your own backyard to be treated. You wouldn't want someone digging big ruts in your backyard, dumping their trash in your driveway, or getting crazy and running all over your bushes and tearing down your trees, would you? Well, the same goes for the outdoor experience. The outdoors are a resource that we all share, and respecting it is the best way to enjoy it.

Of course, we racers do get a little competitive from time to time, and sometimes we need to help convince someone they should help us out. One time, we were racing in Baja, headed to La Paz. Just 20 miles into the race—somewhere outside of Ensenada—I ran into a big problem. The distributor drive gear in

>> below: **Respect the outdoors and treat it the way you would want your own backyard treated.** opposite: **When driving off road, tread lightly! While you may think your vehicle will have only a small impact on an area, years of vehicles abusing the same spots can spoil the fun for everyone.** *Ken Brubaker*

CHAPTER 3: THE OFF-ROAD ADVENTURER'S CODE

>> **Beware of rock-slides and other obstacles you may encounter when driving on the trail.** *Ken Brubaker*

CHAPTER 3: THE OFF-ROAD ADVENTURER'S CODE

I'm often asked where I got the name "Ironman." I can tell you it wasn't because of my lead foot, although I did drive pretty fast a lot of the time. And it wasn't because I had a cast iron stomach, although I have eaten some interesting things during some of my own off-road adventures—especially in Baja.

Truth be told, back in the mid-1970s Valvoline Oil Company created something called the Valvoline Ironman trophy. Valvoline's plan was to give the Ironman trophy to anybody who could drive the Baja 500 or Baja 1000 solo. This was a very big deal back then. Today, a lot of people will sign up to drive the Baja 500 or 1000 solo, but they actually have a co-driver. Most off-road racing vehicles today—including the Trophy Trucks and the big buggies and more—have two seats. But in the 1970s, driving solo in the Baja 500 or 1000 meant driving all by yourself.

Of course, the possibility of being the first to win the Ironman trophy just made me want that award even more. I also wanted the $500 prize that came with it and I didn't want to have to split it with a co-driver. Before I competed, I had to convince the guy that owned the race car that I could do it by myself. Because I didn't have a co-driver, if I got a rock in my eye or if I got sick, tired, or hurt, that would be the end of the race—not just for me, but for the owner of the vehicle too. That was a risk that few owners back then were willing to take, and I can't really blame them.

As it turned out, I was the first person to drive the Baja 1000 solo in a single-seat vehicle. I was also the first racer to win the Ironman trophy in the Baja 1000. I also won the Ironman trophy twice in the Baja 500. The Ironman trophy and I became close friends, and the name just sort of rubbed off on me. I became the Ironman. Before I knew it, my sponsor Toyota realized that they had a unique opportunity to show potential customers that their products were as tough as anything Ford or Chevy could put together, so they started using the Ironman name in their truck advertising. Once that happened, my new name—Ivan "Ironman" Stewart—was set in stone.

---

my engine wasn't compatible with the cam gear. The gears didn't mesh, and the engine wasn't firing right. If I was going to make it all the way to La Paz, I needed to get the right gear—and fast—but that's not the kind of spare part I would typically carry with me, and my crew was a long ways away.

So, with no obvious help in sight, I decided to take things into my own hands. I hurried over to a spectator's truck, lifted up his hood, and took his distributor out. He ran over and said, "Hey, what are you doing?" I replied, "I'm taking your distributor—I need your distributor gear."

As you can imagine, a heated conversation followed. "I'm going to take it," I told him. "NO!" he replied. Then I said, "Either I'm going to take it or we're going to have one hell of a fight!"

I pulled out his distributor and, as it turned out, it was the wrong gear—he had a 302 and I had a 351 Windsor. I put the distributor back in his truck and he was fine. I did eventually get another one—the

right one—and I was all set. We went down another 40 miles or so to a little town called Valle Trinidad, and my coil failed. This was a disastrous race, and I was none too pleased with the way it was going so far. But here's the funny part. The same guy I had borrowed the distributor from outside of Ensenada had gone down the course and ended up at Valle Trinidad—and he was at the exact same spot where I lost my coil.

I took his coil and continued the race.

I wish that was the last of the problems I had in that race, but it wasn't. We blew a head gasket and I ended up putting seawater in the radiator to keep the engine from overheating—something I definitely do not recommend except in the case of an absolute emergency. But, guess what? We ended up persevering and finished the race. We didn't get first place, but we did win the overall championship for Class 8 trucks that year by just a point or two. By keeping in the race—and finishing it—we stayed in the running

for the big prize. Anybody can quit, but what do you get if you quit? Nothing. Winning becomes habit forming. It's the same in whatever you do—in business, in life, and in winning races.

TREAD LIGHTLY!

A great organization called Tread Lightly! is dedicated to educating outdoor adventurers on ways to enjoy the great outdoors without causing irreparable harm to the plants and animals that live there full-time. The best off-road adventures are ones that take you to an amazing place you've never seen before while respecting the people, plants, and animals that live there. The less of an impact you make on your way through, the more future visitors will get to enjoy the special place you just experienced for yourself.

On its website (www.treadlightly.org), Tread Lightly! offers the following specific tips to offroaders:

TRAVEL AND RECREATE
WITH MINIMUM IMPACT

- Stay on designated routes.

- Travel only in areas open to four-wheeling.

- Know your vehicle's limitations. When in doubt, re-track.

- For your safety, travel straight up or down hills. Don't traverse the face of a hill; you may slip sideways or roll your vehicle.

- Cross large rocks and other obstacles slowly, at an angle, one wheel at a time.

- When possible, avoid mud. In soft terrain, go easy on the gas to avoid wheel-spin, which can cause rutting.

- Cross ravines slowly at a 45-degree angle.

>> **In National Forests, new legislation has made the trails available to ORVs restricted to designated trails. If there is no sign in a national forest, you may not be able to drive there.**
Lee Klancher

- Straddle ruts, gullies, and washouts even if they are wider than your vehicle.

- Cross streams only at designated fording points, or where the road crosses the stream.

- Don't turn around on narrow roads, steep terrain, or unstable ground. Backup until you find a safe place to turn around.

- Stop frequently and reconnoiter ahead on foot.

- Avoid riding in meadows and marshy areas.

- Go easy on the throttle and avoid riding the brake or clutch.

- To help with traction, balance your load and lower tire pressure to where you see a bulge (typically not less than 20 pounds).

- Know where the differential or lowest point on the vehicle is.

- Choose the appropriate winch for your vehicle size.

- Attach towing cable, tree strap, or chain as low as possible to the object being winched. Let the winch do the work; never drive the winch.

- Protect the soundscape by avoiding unnecessary noise created by your vehicle.

- Practice minimum impact camping by using established sites, camping 200 feet from water resources and trails, and minimizing use of fire.

- Observe proper sanitary waste disposal by burying waste 6 to 8 inches deep and at least 200 feet from trails, campsites, and water resources. Or, pack out your waste.

RESPECT THE ENVIRONMENT AND THE RIGHTS OF OTHERS

- Be considerate of others on the road or trail.

- Drive only where permitted.

- Leave gates as you find them. Respect private land.

- Yield the right-of-way to those passing you or traveling uphill. Yield to mountain bikers, hikers, and horses.

- Keep the noise and dust down.

- Pack out what you pack in.

>> **Buckle up! Seat belts don't just help keep you safe in the event of an accident, they make your driving position more stable, giving you more control over your vehicle.** *Rick Shandley*

EDUCATE YOURSELF, PLAN, AND PREPARE BEFORE YOU GO

- Obtain a map of your destination and determine which areas are open to off-highway vehicles.

- Contact the land manager for area restrictions, closures, and permit requirements. If you cross private property, be sure to ask permission from the landowner(s).

- Make a realistic plan and stick to it. Always tell someone where you are going and your expected return time.

- Check the weather forecast.

- Make sure your vehicle is mechanically up to task. Be prepared with tools, supplies, and spares for trailside repairs.

- Prepare for the unexpected by packing necessary emergency items.

- Travel with a group of two or more vehicles, as riding solo can leave you vulnerable if you have an accident or breakdown. Designate meeting areas in case of separation.

- Buckle up! Seatbelts are mandatory.

- Know your limitations. Watch your time, your fuel, and your energy.

- Maintain a reasonable distance between vehicles.

- Don't mix driving with alcohol and/or drugs.

- Understand your vehicle's controls and how to operate them.

ALLOW FOR FUTURE USE OF THE OUTDOORS, LEAVE IT BETTER THAN YOU FOUND IT

- Carry a trash bag in you vehicle and pick up litter left by others.

- Ride in the middle of trails to minimize widening of the trails. Avoid sideslipping and wheel spin, which can lead to erosion.

- Avoid "spooking" livestock and wildlife.

- Always avoid sensitive habitats: wetlands, meadows, and tundra.

- Following a ride, wash your vehicle to reduce the spread of noxious weeds.

- Motorized and mechanized vehicles are not allowed in designated wilderness areas.

DISCOVER THE REWARDS OF RESPONSIBLE RECREATION

- Four-wheeling provides the opportunity to get away from the rush of everyday life and builds family traditions.

- Careless operation of your off-highway vehicle can cause damage and may result in the closing of an area.

- Respect the environment and other trail users. By using common sense and common courtesy, what is available today will be here to enjoy tomorrow.

>> **Ride in the middle of trails and avoid the temptation to run off the beaten track.**
Rick Shandley

DRIVING SKILLS

A key part of enjoying the off-road experience is knowing what you're doing when you get there. Should you or shouldn't you cross that innocent-looking babbling brook? What should you do when your wheels start spinning in the soft sand? How can you avoid getting sideways on a hill and thus prevent a potentially dangerous vehicle rollover? In the following chapters, I explain how to approach and successfully deal with the most common off-road challenges and obstacles, from dirt and water, to mud, rocks, and silt—and much more—safely and easily.

BEFORE YOU SET A TIRE OFF ROAD, YOU'VE GOT TO BE

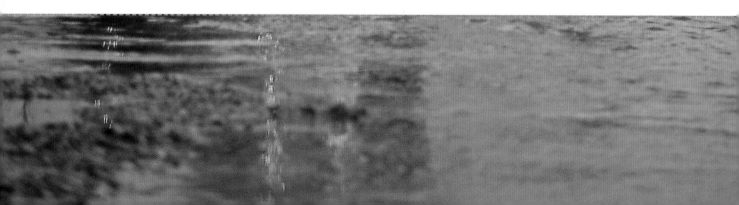

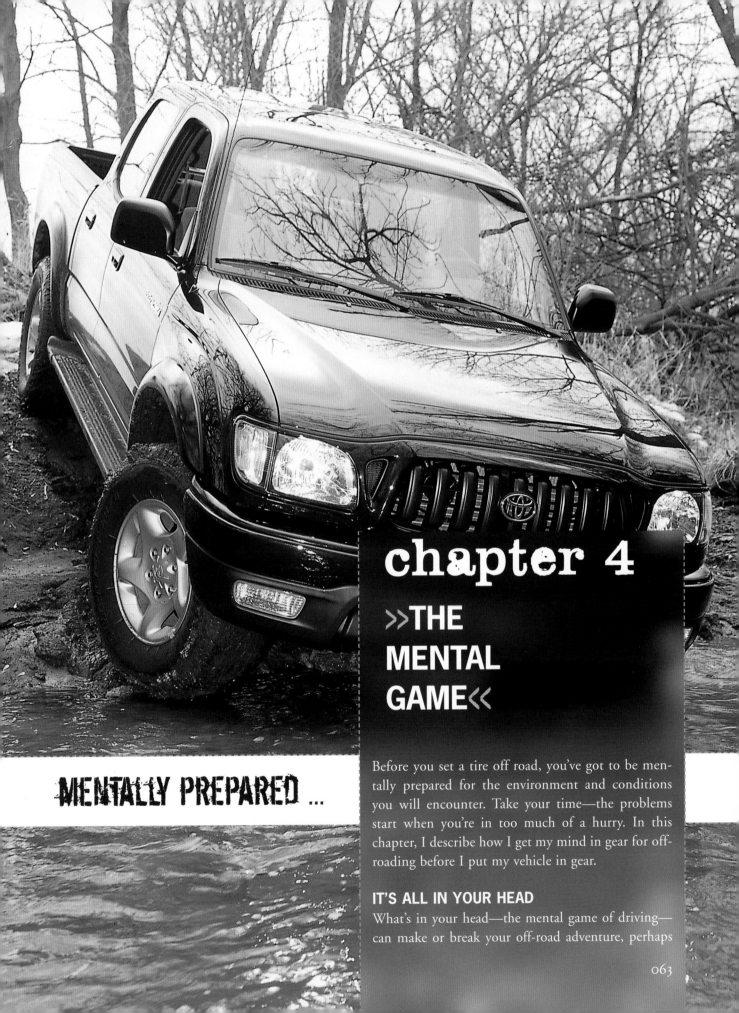

chapter 4

>>THE MENTAL GAME<<

Before you set a tire off road, you've got to be mentally prepared for the environment and conditions you will encounter. Take your time—the problems start when you're in too much of a hurry. In this chapter, I describe how I get my mind in gear for off-roading before I put my vehicle in gear.

IT'S ALL IN YOUR HEAD

What's in your head—the mental game of driving—can make or break your off-road adventure, perhaps

MENTALLY PREPARED ...

PREVIOUS PAGE >> **Left: Some off-road adventures are best approached using only a heavily modified vehicle. Right: Others are just fine using a showroom-stock vehicle without any modifications whatsoever. Know which are which!** *Ken Brubaker*

even more so than the brand of truck you drive, whether or not your rig is lifted, or whether it has big tires and locking differentials. All that stuff is important, but your brain is by far the most important ingredient for a safe and enjoyable off-road adventure. Some of the key aspects of the mental game include:

- Motivation. What's your motivation for going off road? Are you in an adventurous mood? Want to see some new places and meet some new people? Want to show off your hot driving skills to your

new girlfriend? Whatever your motivation is, it will definitely have an impact—good, or maybe bad—on your off-road adventure.

- Attitude. Are you the kind of person who thinks that it's just not fun unless you're leaving big doughnuts and tearing up the ground, or running over bushes and small animals? If that's your attitude, then you've got an attitude problem, and it's going to come back and bite you someday—probably sooner than later.

>> Below/Opposite Left: **Nothing can spoil a great day outdoors quite like a flat tire, a bent tie rod, or some other broken part. While a toolkit can help you get going again in the event of relatively minor problems, major problems may require professional help—or a tow.** *Ken Brubaker*

- Limits. Do you know your limits? Really? Can you set limits and then adhere to them? Knowing and establishing limits is a key ingredient in the mental game.

- Qualities of a good driver. Good drivers share a common set of mental characteristics that go a long way to make them the way they are. They are cool under pressure, they don't get flustered when presented with a challenge, they plan ahead and think about what they are going to do, and they continuously practice and hone their skills. They don't take unnecessary risks, and they know that the process of getting where they want to go is half the fun.

While I can't get inside your head and make you become completely aware of your own mental game, I can tell you that it's something you should become aware of yourself. How you play the mental game is probably the one thing that will make or break your off-road adventure, so take some time to reflect and understand where you're at before you go.

MAKING MISTAKES

Way back in chapter 1, I gave you a bit of advice that I learned the hard way: Don't make mistakes. That's an easy thing to say, but what does it have to do with your mental game, and can you honestly do anything about it?

Consider this mistake: Let's say that you're humming along, and you keep sliding off the side of the dirt road. You know you're doing something wrong, but you're not sure exactly what it is. The mistake is

>> **Cracking your suspension with a big rock is one of many mistakes you can make off road. Know where the bottom of your rig is, and drive around obstacles whenever you can instead of taking them on directly.** *Rick Shandley*

that you're driving outside the parameters of the situation. You're either going too fast, your rig isn't setup for the task, or both. For example, your shocks may be worn out or broken. To take control and stop making this mistake, you've got to get back inside the parameters of the situation by slowing down—maybe way down. You should know exactly where your tires are every inch of the way. A few inches can make the difference between having a great adventure and falling off a cliff, hitting a tree, hitting a big rock, or running over a tire-flattening obstacle.

When I was driving my $500,000 race car off-road, I had to know exactly where my tires were at all times. It's the same thing with you driving home after work. If you drift across the double line, you're going to have a problem. I call that a mistake. If you get lost while you're racing, that's called a mistake. If you get stuck in the mud, that's called a mistake.

What's interesting about mistakes is that they apply not only to your off-road adventures, but also to your everyday life. Whether you're running a business or running an off-road race, you need to stay within the parameters. You can only afford to go so fast in your business because you've only got 'X' amount of budget to work with. You've got to know what your competition is doing, when to accelerate, when to decelerate, when to spend money on marketing, and when to spend money on better tires. You need more horsepower but you can't afford more horsepower, so you'd better drive within the parameters you've got.

It's a great philosophy, and it's given me the confidence to do so many things over the years. I've learned how to win, and I have also learned how to lose. I hate losing with a passion, but it goes hand-in-hand with the mental game of getting out of your comfort zone. I tell people all the time that I look at winning or losing very personally. I absolutely love to win, but I hate to lose more than I love to win. It's easy to make excuses about why you lost—too hot, too cold, not enough schooling—but the guy who actually accomplished his goal and made it happen did so because he stuck with it, persevered, and overcame the challenges in his way.

Don't get me wrong. I fail all the time. We all do. I'm not afraid of failure, but I do not like it. Competing accelerates your learning. It has to

because most of us don't want to lose, and we work harder to win.

A good example of making mistakes came when I was racing with Charlotte Corral in the Baja 1000. We left Ensenada early in the morning of the race and headed south. Right off, we had a lot of troubles. The alternator went out, the battery went dead, and on and on and on. We had raced all day long and all night long, and only got halfway to our destination. Twenty-four hours into the race, we were only down to about San Ignacio. When we finally did get to San Ignacio—an area with lots of lagoons and silt—the fog rolled in. It's already kind of an eerie place because you can get stuck really easily, and you can get turned around and end up lost. That fog really put the icing on that big, creepy cake.

I was really tired after 24 hours of racing, but I started to get this nagging feeling that things weren't right. As we were (I thought) headed south towards La Paz, I realized that the sun was rising on my right side. Even though I was tired, it didn't take much to figure out I was going the wrong way. So I started to slow down. Charlotte was sitting next to me, and she said, "What are you going so slow for?" I said, "Charlotte, why is the sun rising over there? We're going north!" I had made a big mistake. I let my fatigue and all our little mishaps get the better of me. We lost that race.

Sal Fish, a long-time friend of mine who owns SCORE International Off-Road Racing, was marking an off-road race course when his transmission failed way out in the middle of nowhere. Sal's transmission went out because he was jerking the drive train, trying to get unstuck from some rut or hole. He didn't think about what he was doing or about the possible impact of his decisions before he started jerking his truck around. Sure enough, his transmission broke, and if that wasn't bad enough, he was 40 miles away from any kind of help. He managed to get himself deeply into trouble.

DON'T MAKE IT WORSE!

The moral of Sal's story is, once you've gotten yourself in trouble, don't make it worse! That can be hard to avoid. We want to get back on the road again as quickly as we can, so we end up pushing the situation too hard and making a mistake that's even worse. During the course of my racing career, I was really fortunate when it came to avoiding trouble. I always managed to get myself out, and I never spent the night broken down out in the desert. After hearing so many stories about drivers having problems, I definitely didn't want to spend the night freezing in the rain or walking across 20 miles of hot sand to get help.

We all make mistakes. The idea is to learn from them and to try not to repeat them. When somebody asks, "How do you have a safe and enjoyable off-road adventure?" My answer is: Don't make mistakes—at least not big ones that will put you, your passengers, or your rig in danger of serious injury or damage. If you do make a mistake, as we all do, don't make it worse by compounding that mistake with other—potentially more serious—ones.

So, if you feel yourself sliding off the road, for example, be in tune with what's happening and take corrective action. In that case, the right kind of corrective action would be to slow down—gently and gradually—because you're going too fast. The wrong kind of corrective action would be to go even faster, or to slow down quickly by slamming your brakes, potentially resulting in an out-of-control spin. Don't make it worse!

If you feel the suspension bottoming out on your SUV, first of all, be in tune with it, and consider exactly what is going on. Your vehicle is telling you it isn't built to handle the kind of challenge you're throwing at it. Just because you're driving an SUV doesn't mean it's built to tackle especially rugged off-road challenges. Many SUVs are far more show than go. The

>> **If you find yourself getting dug deeper and deeper into the sand, don't make it worse! Stop doing what you're doing, take time to evaluate your situation, and then do something different.** *Rick Shandley*

CHAPTER 4: THE MENTAL GAME

right kind of corrective action would be to slow down and find a gentler route through the area, or turn back. The wrong kind of corrective action would be to keep doing what you're doing—digging a deeper hole and increasing your chances of compounding your relatively minor errors with some very serious ones. Don't make it worse! When you start banging the suspension, chances are you're going to break something and get stuck. Then what are you going to do?

THE COMFORT ZONE

We all have a place where we are comfortable with our own skills and experience, with the equipment we are driving, and with the locations and challenges we plan to encounter in our journeys. This place is our comfort zone, and it usually determines the kinds of driving challenges we are willing to take on. When you feel yourself getting outside your comfort zone, that should be a warning that you're about to make a mistake, and this mistake can be easily compounded if you take the wrong kind of corrective action. I can tell you from personal experience that getting out of your comfort zone is exciting. There's nothing quite like the surge of adrenalin you get when you know you're riding on the razor-sharp edge just this side of disaster, but that feeling also indicates you're potentially setting yourself up to make a big mistake.

Be aware of your comfort zone and don't push it too far too fast.

When I first got my driver's license, I couldn't wait to go to my buddy's house only two blocks away to show him I had reached that important milestone in my life, but I wasn't comfortable driving a real car yet—a go-cart, yes, but a real car, no. So, I drove directly to his house, showed him my car, and drove right back home. That was it. I stayed firmly within my comfort zone. Eventually, I started getting a little more adventurous, and I decided to drive to downtown El Cajon, California, which at the time was about the same size as downtown Mayberry, and expand my comfort zone a little further. I eventually got onto the freeway and started driving at night. Before long, I could drive anywhere, anytime. Slowly

073

but surely, I expanded my comfort zone as I got more practice driving and more confident in my skills.

We all do the same thing. For you, a trip to a local off-road park might be within your comfort zone, and then you say, "Let's go to Baja!" In Baja, you'll encounter challenges far greater than in your local off-road park—challenges that will potentially take you far outside your comfort zone and introduce the possibility of making some very big mistakes. By all means, have fun and enjoy the new challenges you'll encounter along the way, but try not to make mistakes. You're going to hit a rock, and maybe have a flat, but don't make it worse. Don't keep driving on it until you have a really major problem that won't be so easy to repair or resolve.

Here's something else to think about: Whenever you break down, or get into a serious problem, you have an obligation to take your situation very seriously. Don't make it worse by being polite and thinking to yourself, "I don't want to put anybody out." I've seen bad situations get much worse in off-road racing when someone didn't ask for help—didn't demand it—when they really needed it. If you're hurt and bleeding, or out of water, or need a fire extinguisher or a tug out of a mud puddle, then don't be shy. Get out there and ask for help.

WHAT'S THE RUSH?
TAKE TIME TO SMELL THE ROSES

Any time you hurry, whether you are rushing to get to dinner, fix a flat tire, or drive across country, your odds for having some sort of problem increase. That's another part of the off-road equation: Don't hurry. It's not a race.

I got a ticket going from Tucson to San Diego a while ago because I decided that I was going to set a personal record from Tucson to my house. I got a ticket for driving 105 miles an hour. It was stupid. In California, the penalty for driving that fast is the same as the penalty for a DUI, and the sad thing about it was that after the officer started to write the ticket, he said, "Oh, you're not the same Ivan "Ironman" Stewart who off-road races, are you?" and I thought, "Why didn't you pick up on that before you started writing the ticket?" By then it was too late, and he had to give it to me.

Of course, if I hadn't been in such a rush in the first place, I wouldn't have made that mistake. As soon as you get off road, there won't be any signs out there. There won't be anybody to help you if you stub your toe—except a buddy, if you brought one along—and there won't be somebody to get an ambulance if you get in even worse trouble. You'll be on your own, and that's something you have to always keep in mind. The last thing you want to do is get hurt out there and need stitches, and have to make a three-hour ride to a hospital somewhere.

So, engage your brain, take it easy, but don't forget to have fun, too! That's one of the main reasons you decided to go off-road adventuring, right?

Which reminds me of one time when I had some fun with my co-driver on a lonely night in Baja. Visualize this for a minute: It's summertime, and you're afraid of snakes, so you don't particularly want to walk around at night because that's when the snakes come out of their daytime hiding places to look for a bite to eat. However, because this is Baja, you're out in the middle of nowhere, it's dark, and—as you're driving—you come across literally hundreds of barbwire fences to keep the cattle where they're supposed to be. For every barbwire fence, there's a lousy little barbwire gate that goes across the road. You see these all around Baja, and when there's one blocking the road you're driving on, you've got to stop your vehicle, get out, open the gate, drive through, and close the gate again.

No problem. Unless it's dark, you're afraid of snakes, and you're the guy who's got the job of getting out of the truck to open and close the gate.

So, one night I was prerunning through Baja with my co-driver Frank Arciero Jr. and he was the designated gate opener and closer, and he had to do this over and over because we'd get through a gate, then go another mile or so and come to another gate. Then we'd go another five miles and encounter another gate. We had to pull up close to the gates because you don't want the rancher's livestock to get out. But this particular night, I decided to have a little fun with Frank.

I started talking about all the dangerous rattlesnakes that hang out where we were driving, and how they are all over the place at night, looking for something good to eat. I knew he was terrified of snakes. One time his wife chased him around with a garter snake she picked up, and I was sure he'd jump out of his pants. So I'm setting him up, telling him, "You really got to watch these snakes out here. Here we are way out in the middle of nowhere so if you ever got bit by a snake, it would be a bad deal."

So, I pulled up to a gate and Frank carefully stepped out like he always did—checking to be sure he didn't step on a snake. He unlocked and opened the gate while I drove through, but this time when I stopped to wait for him to get back in the car, I put on the emergency brake and slipped out of the car while he was back there locking the gate and fiddling around. This was 2 o'clock in the morning, and you couldn't easily see inside the car from the outside. I came around and hid behind his open door. When he stepped back in the cab, I reached over and pinched him really hard on the leg. I scared him so much I thought he was going to jump over the car and go running off into the night. After he realized that I was the snake, we both got a good laugh out of that one.

... ITS A GOOD IDEA TO RUN THROUGH SOME BASIC

OFF-ROAD DRIVING SKILLS

chapter 5

>>BASIC OFF-ROAD DRIVING SKILLS<<

You can probably tackle plenty of low-key off-road driving adventures without having any special driving skills beyond those you have acquired from driving on regular, paved roads. Nonetheless, it's a good idea to run through some basic off-road driving skills you'll need when the going gets rough. In this chapter, we cover some fundamentals. If you've already got the basic skills under your belt, go ahead and jump to chapter 6 where we cover advanced off-road driving skills.

FIRST, A FEW RULES

- Use common sense when driving your vehicle. I shouldn't have to say that, but you'd be surprised how many people leave their common sense at home with the pet dog.

- Consider the laws of nature and gravity while driving. They have not been suspended (at least the last time I checked).

- Be aware of what is around you and where your vehicle's tires are placed to anticipate where the vehicle is heading.

- In a problem area, always keep one vehicle clear in solid terrain (assuming you brought a buddy or two with you) so it is available to come to the assistance if the other vehicle becomes stuck.

- Don't follow too close to the vehicle in front of you, and leave enough room to stop if the vehicle in front of you stops. This is especially important in dusty, dark, foggy, or other low-visibility conditions where you can't see very far ahead.

GETTING YOURSELF IN THE RIGHT POSITION

As the driver of your vehicle, you are the most important part of the off-road driving experience. That being the case, it's important to get properly setup and in the right place in your vehicle to maximize your visibility and to ensure you have total command of your vehicle—at least as much command as someone can have over two or three tons of steel, plastic, and gasoline!

>> **Before you get going, adjust your seat...**
...and your mirrors *Rick Shandley*

SEATING POSITION

For the best visibility, sit up as high as you can. Be comfortable. Adjust your seat to a position that causes your arms and legs to be slightly bent and where you can reach all of the important controls without stretching. Your left foot should be placed on the floor to the left of the brake (what we call the "dead pedal" area) for support. Seat belts and shoulder harnesses are very effective in keeping

>> **Plan your best route and then execute it. But be prepared to adjust it quickly in the event that conditions are not as you anticipated.** *Ken Brubaker*

drivers in their seats and thus in control at all times, both of which are key ingredients to safe off-roading.

STEERING WHEEL

Keep two hands on the steering wheel. When you are not shifting, your hands should rest on the wheel at 2 or 3 o'clock and 9 or 10 o'clock. What happens when you hit a rut going 30 miles an hour? Your steering wheel will try to jerk its way out of your hands as your tires snap into place. More than a few off-roaders have injured their thumbs when this happens. Keep thumbs up and outside the steering wheel to prevent damage in case your steering wheel is jarred from your hands in a severe off-road situation. Normally, with power steering, you won't have to keep too tight a grip on the steering wheel, but when driving off road, you may need to go with a tighter grip. Remember: the tighter your grip on the wheel, the less you will be able to tell what your tires are doing.

THE BOTTOM LINE

We react to what we see, what we hear, and what we feel. If you've ever heard the saying "driving by the seat of your pants," it's really true. The contact we have with the seat and pedals gives us information about what the vehicle is doing. When we grip the steering wheel, we are getting information directly from the tires, telling us where they are pointed, how well they are gripping, and if they are getting ready to break loose. Ultimately, we are tire managers, and it's our responsibility to keep traction on all of our tires.

Be alert to your surroundings. One of the competitors in our Baja Protruck Racing Series got hurt in an off-road racing accident in a dune buggy. He's severely

>> **Keep two hands on the steering wheel at all times!**

burned, but he still loves off-road racing. He can't drive anymore because of the extent of his injuries, but he happily rides along. For some reason, I think his injuries actually made him stronger in other ways. His senses are so good that, while riding along out in the middle of Baja, he picked up on a weird sound from the engine that was barely audible. After he began hearing the sound, he noticed that the oil pressure light was flickering. He and the driver stopped and got out of the car to investigate. Sure enough, they soon realized that oil was pouring out of the pan. The oil drain plug had come out. Luckily, they caught it just in time and didn't ruin the engine. One of the guys felt around under the skid plate and found the oil plug. They put the plug back in, poured oil in the engine, and continued the race.

Everybody uses a different seating position. As long as you are comfortable; can clearly see and reach all the controls; and have a good line of sight out the windshield, windows, and mirrors—go with it!

UNDERSTANDING VEHICLE DYNAMICS

Your vehicle is always in one of two states. It's either static (not moving) or dynamic (moving). When we're driving, we are more interested in vehicle dynamics—how the vehicle is going to respond to the many different inputs it gets as you move down the road. When your right front tire hits a pothole, what's it going to do? Will your suspension easily soak up the shock, or will it jerk your steering wheel out of your hands and throw you into the bushes? When you hit a patch of gravel, how will your brakes react when you give them a sudden tap?

>> **The more you practice driving off-road, the better you'll get at feeling the limits of your vehicle, such as when your tires start to slide on an icy track.** *Ken Brubaker*

>> **This is one sure way to see what it feels like to bottom out your suspension. Although it looks like fun, we don't recommend following this example.** *Ken Brubaker*

the speed of the vehicle. This could require additional throttle—don't add too much, though—to keep the wheels spinning at the proper vehicle speed when your tires come back in contact with the ground. Remember, your vehicle is not equipped to fly, and some landings can be harmful to your health and the health of your rig!

- We are tire managers! As drivers, our main responsibility is to manage the part of the tire making contact with the ground, called the tire contact patch. Each tire patch is about the size of your hand. We are constantly getting information from contact with our driver seat, pedals, and steering wheel as to how much or how little traction each tire has.

- The four contact patches. The part of the tire that makes contact with the ground is the contact patch. The control of your vehicle will be determined by how you react to the messages received from your four contact patches. Every time you brake, go around a corner, or even accelerate, the contact patches change shape and size. When you accelerate, the contact patches grow bigger in the rear and get smaller in front because weight is transferred to the rear of the vehicle. Upon braking, the front tire patches get larger while the ones at the rear get smaller, again due to weight transfer. When cornering, the outside tire patches grow larger while the inside tire patches become smaller. It's what you do and how well you understand what the contact patches are telling you that enable you to maintain maximum

>> **We are tire managers!** *Rick Shandley*

vehicle control and find—and stay within—the limits of your vehicle.

THE RIDE OF A LIFETIME

Years ago, when I was a superintendent for the Atlas Fence Company in San Diego, I was getting ready to drive in the Baja 1000. One of the guys who worked for me—he was just 18 years old at the time—asked me if it was okay to take the day off and watch the start of the race. I said, "Sure, no problem." So at about 5 o'clock in the afternoon, Coco Corral—my co-rider for the race—called me at the Hotel San Nicolas and he said, "I've got some bad news, I'm not going to be able to make the race." I was supposed to drive the first 500 miles of the race while he watched the road and helped me work on the car. Then he was going to get out of the car and Charlotte was going to get in. We would finish, winning the Baja 1000 and the championship. At least that was the game plan.

When I got that call from Coco, I could see my shot at winning the Baja 1000—and championship—evaporate like a drop of water on a hot rock in the desert right before my eyes. My race truck was ready to go, we had our pit stops arranged and setup all the way down the Baja peninsula, I had gas supplies staged where I would need them, and I had my entire support crew in place. Coco also had the cash we needed to pay for unanticipated expenses along the way.

There was already a lot of time and money tied up in this race—not to mention the championship—and Coco wasn't going to be able to make it. That was definitely not going to work for me. So I hurried out into Ensenada and

>> **While catching air is a lot of fun, remember that those landings can be tough on your rig. Is yours built to last?** *Ken Brubaker*

found my employee walking down the street. I said, "What are you doing tomorrow?" He said, "I've got to go back to work," and I said, "No, you get another day off. How would you like to race the Baja 1000 with me down to La Paz?" He said, "You bet! Let me call my mom." I said, "Okay, hurry up and call your mom—we've got to get you a driver's suit and a helmet, get you signed up, get you an arm band, and all the rest of the stuff."

We took off from the starting line, and it was a really tough race. I had one heck of a time staying awake. We had all kinds of trouble with the engine and I had to trade my sweatshirt for a battery, but we made to La Paz. We finished in fifth place, and we won the Class 8 Championship by just one point. After the race was over and the celebrations were enjoyed and survived, we needed to get back to Ensenada. The trouble was that I had a ticket for a flight back, but my employee didn't, so now he was stuck down there.

We took him with us to the airport in La Paz, and we went out on the runway. In those days, you used to get on an airplane through a ramp in the back of the plane as well as through another door in the front. This was back in the 1970s and security wasn't like it is today. There was a crowd of people milling around the airplane, jockeying to get on board and grab seats. I talked my employee into slipping in the door and acting like he had a ticket. He mingled with the people in the back of the airplane, walked in with the paying passengers, and sat down. Nobody checked his ticket, which was a good thing because he didn't have one, and he made it back to Ensenada with no problem.

EYE TECHNIQUES

When it comes to driving, your eyes are the most important part of your body. Your ability to focus on situations quickly and use your eyes properly can be the difference between avoiding a bad situation or adding to it. You can actually exercise and train your eyes to do this.

We tend to go where we look. Keep your eyes up and look as far ahead as you need to so you can make proper decisions on a timely basis. If you veer off the road or into the rough, look at where you want to go. Have focal points—something to aim for. Above all, do not look at what you are going to run into, or—guess what—you will run into it.

- Trust your peripheral vision: Be aware of the "big picture."

- Night driving: Don't overdrive your headlights.

- Eye fatigue: If your eyes are tired, this may not be the best time to drive.

You react to what you see. Use your eyes properly. Look ahead and know what your objectives are so you have enough time to make proper decisions, but also keep an eye to the sides, and learn to use and trust your peripheral vision.

BRAKING TECHNIQUES

At its very heart, braking is primarily an exercise in weight transfer. The ability to reduce your speed is not only related to how good your brakes are but also how well you keep your tires in contact with the ground. Braking hard tends to reduce the traction on the rear tires as the weight of the vehicle shifts forward, reducing overall braking effectiveness. This may also cause you to lose control of the vehicle. If the vehicle is already light in the back, such as a pickup truck with an empty cargo bed, transferring the weight to the front tires in braking can cause the rear wheels to completely lose traction, break loose, and spin the car around.

Correct brake pressure requires a lot of sensitivity between your foot and the brake pedal. I recommend that you use the ball of your right foot on the brake pedal. This allows the maximum sensitivity and leverage to reduce the speed of your vehicle. In racing conditions, every millisecond of reaction time counts, so I actually used to rest my left foot on the brake pedal, where it was always ready for action.

Under normal circumstances, you do not want to lock up the brakes. Whenever possible, avoid slamming on the brakes. Unless you've got ABS, hitting the brakes too hard will likely upset the balance of your vehicle or cause wheel lock-up—or both—resulting in loss of control.

REAR WHEEL LOCK-UP

Rear wheel lock-up most often occurs on downhill turns where there is minimal weight on the rear wheels. To control rear wheel lock-up, you must have the steering wheel straight, while reducing your braking pressure until the wheels unlock. If the rear wheels lock up with any turn on the steering wheel, the rear end may come around so fast, you may not be able to react in time, and end up spinning out.

FRONT WHEEL LOCK-UP

When your front wheels lock up, you lose the ability to steer your vehicle. This is not a good thing. When this happens, turning the steering wheel will not change the direction of your vehicle. Your vehicle will go straight or in the direction it was going before the wheels locked up. To get control of the situation, you must reduce the pressure on your brake pedal until the wheels unlock (if your vehicle is not equipped with ABS). Your tires must rotate for you to have directional control.

ABS (Antilock Braking System)

If you have a vehicle equipped with ABS and apply max-imum brake pressure, the sensors will activate when they sense wheel lock up. The ABS will unlock the wheel that is locked to allow it to rotate. As we've already seen, tires must rotate to have directional control. Your ABS will "unlock-lock" the wheels approximately 15 to 30 times per second, depending upon the type of system. This causes pulsating of the brake pedal and is fairly noisy. When you activate your ABS and want to continue to reduce your speed, keep firm and constant pressure on the brake pedal. Do not pump the brakes! Pumping the brakes keeps the ABS from doing its job. The noise and pulsation of the brake pedal are normal.

SELECTING THE RIGHT GEAR

Using the appropriate gear is also helpful in keeping the tires on the ground and, therefore, keeping total control of your

>> **Different terrain will affect how your vehicle reacts to your steering (and braking) inputs. Know where the limits are—and be sure you stay within them!** *Rick Shandley*

|CHAPTER 5: BASIC OFF-ROAD DRIVING SKILLS

>> **A good mud tire can get you into—and back out of—places where a regular tire wouldn't dare tread.** *Ken Brubaker*

>> **Water hazards can be particulary challenging—and dangerous.** *Ken Brubaker*

vehicle. By putting the vehicle in the proper gear before you get stuck, you can avoid getting stuck altogether.

If you are going to climb a steep hill, using a lower gear will allow you to climb the hill while maintaining enough power to climb smoothly and steadily throughout the entire ascent. If you were to climb that same hill in a higher gear, your vehicle speed would have to be much faster to maintain enough engine rpm to crest the hill. If there are ruts halfway up the hill, at a higher speed in a higher gear you could lose traction or control when you are in the ruts.

- Choosing the best gear will give you overall better vehicle response and acceleration abilities.

- Choosing the lower gear also enables you to utilize engine compression to help slow your vehicle when you let off the gas instead of using your brakes. This helps keep your brakes cool and ready for when you really need them.

- Altitude is a consideration for power. The higher the altitude, the lower the gear.

- Using a lower than normal gear allows the engine to keep the vehicle speed slowed to an in-control, drivable level. Then, if you still need more stopping power you have all your brakes available to you as well.

- Driving down a long grade and slowing the vehicle using only the brakes is a very bad practice. It can cause the brakes to overheat, thus becoming less effective, and possibly not effective enough to stop the vehicle in certain situations.

READING THE TERRAIN

Different types of terrain make your vehicle react differently. Ruts may cause the vehicle to react in a way that does not allow you to anticipate the vehicle's movement, while washboard roads give the vehicle a skating feeling, making the vehicle less controllable. Speed—excess speed—is the top cause of problems in off-road driving (or in on-road driving, for that matter). But speed is relative to the situation and terrain you are in. Most four-wheel drive vehicles are designed for climbing over rugged terrain and maintaining traction in a wide variety of challenging road conditions, not for going fast. Going too fast

over the crest or rise of a hill can result in a collision with another vehicle, and is a common cause of suspension damage when the front end comes down hard.

KNOW YOUR LIMITS AND THE LIMITS OF YOUR VEHICLE!

The easiest way of determining if you are driving within your limits is to try to place the vehicle in a certain attitude, at a specific point on the road. If you cannot put the front tires exactly where you want them to go, you are driving too fast for the situation.

Mud, sand, snow, and ice provide a slippery feeling where you can no longer control traction and acceleration—stopping, starting, turning, and braking. Sand will affect your ability to control your vehicle, too, and, like mud, it can get your vehicle stuck. A constant, steady throttle through mud or sand is the best bet. No sharp turns or radical maneuvering. Choose a lower gear before you enter, and try to avoid having to brake. Try to avoid rapid acceleration and use a smooth throttle.

In sand, you can lower your tire pressure to broaden the contact patch of the tire and create a larger footprint—thus obtaining more flotation and traction surface available to the vehicle. We'll get into more detail about how to handle these different driving conditions in subsequent chapters.

A RACING LIFE

I didn't start racing until I was 27 years old. I was married and had three kids, and I couldn't afford race cars. A friend of mine by the name of Bill Hrynko called me in the middle of 1972 and said, "Ivan, I'm going to build a Chenoweth two-seat buggy race car. I will fund it, and if you will help me work on it, you can ride with me." We ran some races with Bill driving and me riding along. I absolutely hated it. I felt I had more natural ability, and I could do a better job.

So we entered the Ensenada 300. Bill was signed up as the driver of record, and I was going to co-drive. Bill called me and said, "I've got bad news. I fell off a ladder at the house and broke my leg. You're going to have to drive." I ended up recruiting a kid by the name of Earl Stahl to ride with me. As we were driving, the throttle wire broke. What a way to start a racing career! But as the old saying goes, necessity is the mother of invention. There was no way I was going to let a little problem like having no throttle mess up my first race as a driver. We took the throttle wire and put it around a

PREVIOUS PAGE >> **Get out of your vehicle and take a close look at the road ahead. What kinds of obstacles are ahead? What's the best path to take?** *Ken Brubaker*

wrench so I could rev the engine with my right hand, while I steered with my left hand.

So far, so good, but there was a problem: I couldn't shift because to do that meant I would have to drop my makeshift throttle lever to the floor, inviting further disaster. So I had Earl do the shifting while I worked the clutch and the brake with my feet. Believe it or not, we ended up winning the race.

After that first win in 1974, Bill Hrynko and I started to do really well. We won some races and got some recognition. Bill would always sign up as the driver of record, but in the championship, the driver of record didn't actually have to drive. Before each race he'd say,

"Why don't you go ahead and start? You do the first half, and then halfway through we'll switch and I'll drive the second half." We probably participated in eight or nine races that year, and we'd get halfway through the race—to the point where Bill was supposed to take over driving duties from me—and he'd say, "Keep going. You're doing good. Keep going." I wound up being the driver throughout all of the races that year.

We did very well. Bill won the driver's championship in 1974 as our driver of record, and he never drove an inch. After that, I think they changed the rules where you had to at least start the race. Shortly after that, I got a call from Modern Motors to drive a single-seat car,

>> **Once you've committed to your plan, don't let up. A moment of doubt can mean a stalled-out rig, and a slow trip downstream.** *Ken Brubaker*

which had more prestige and more recognition in the industry. I soon started winning the Valvoline Ironman trophies and slowly worked my way into trucks. I think winning the Ironman award really helped me in my partnership with Toyota.

Participating in the Baja 1000 was an experience I'll never forget. It was huge, it was fantastic. For a lot of the Mexicans along our race route, it's the biggest thing that happens to them that whole year. All these people go out to the race route and stay up all night long and build little campfires by the side of the road at their favorite spot, ditch, turn, or jump. It looks like the whole place is on fire. There's nothing like the feeling of seeing the lights of La Paz at about three or four o'clock in the morning. You've almost made it! You've gone 1,000 miles over dirt roads and rocks, and up and down hills and mountains.

You've been surprised by cattle in the roadway and gates made out of barbwire, and you've managed to avoid head-on collisions with other racers and the booby traps erected by locals looking for a bit of extra excitement.

Once you get up to the top of the mountain above La Paz, you start looking for the lights of the city, but you can't see them yet. Then, just before you crest and start breaking over the ridge top, the lights of La Paz erupt, but you're not there yet. Just because you've run the majority of the race doesn't mean that there's a guarantee you're going to make it all the way to the finish line. Your axle could break or the engine could blow or you could drop a tranny. When you finally do cross the finish line, there's no feeling like it. Just to finish that race is incredible.

... THINGS START TO GET HAIRY OUT THERE

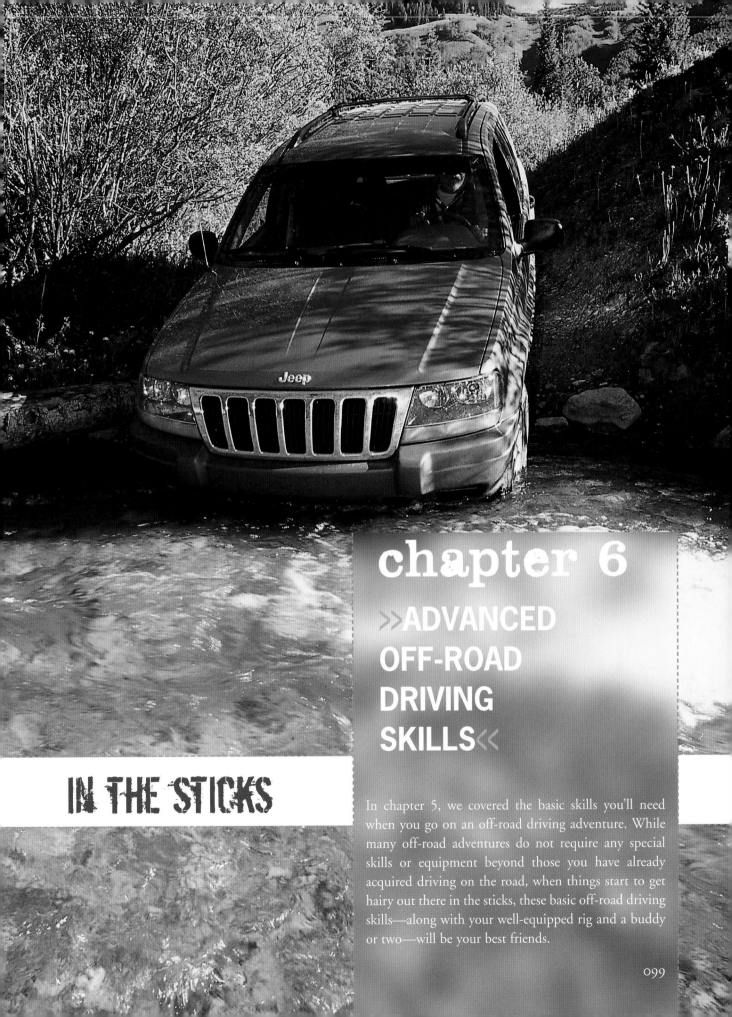

chapter 6

»ADVANCED OFF-ROAD DRIVING SKILLS«

IN THE STICKS

In chapter 5, we covered the basic skills you'll need when you go on an off-road driving adventure. While many off-road adventures do not require any special skills or equipment beyond those you have already acquired driving on the road, when things start to get hairy out there in the sticks, these basic off-road driving skills—along with your well-equipped rig and a buddy or two—will be your best friends.

>>USE SIPDE<<

- **S**can for potential hazards. Look ahead and plan your route. Scanning ahead will allow you to process the information so you can make decisions and execute them.

- **I**dentify hazards and potential situations or conflicts.

- **P**redict what the potential hazards are and how you can best manage them.

- **D**ecide what you need to do based upon your prediction, and chart your course of action. Do you need to adjust your speed, tires, vehicle position, or route?

- **E**xecute your decision.

When you decide you're ready to take on some even more challenging off-road adventures, there are a number of additional advanced off-road topics and driving skills that you should practice before you hit the road.

EYE POSITIONING—LINE OF SIGHT

Scanning the upcoming terrain for obstacles and elements that can affect you or create a potential hazard is a good technique to learn. Scanning includes more than looking at what is in front of you. It also includes keeping an eye on your side and rearview mirrors. Learning to scan also includes getting a sense for where to focus your line of sight. Imagine that you're coming up to a rock that is jutting into the trail. If you keep looking at the rock, chances are you're going to hit it. You want to look at where the tires are going to go, not where you don't want them to go.

Always scan ahead to plan your route of travel, and to have a plan B or escape plan if your line of travel does not work as you had anticipated.

THE KEY TO VEHICLE CONTROL: SMOOTHNESS

Jamming on the brakes, throwing the vehicle into a turn, or jumping on the accelerator too hard may cause the size of the tire patches to change too suddenly or too much, which can cause you to lose control of the vehicle. Take a guess at what happens when you lose control of your vehicle—an off-road adventure that may be quite a bit more exciting than you had planned.

UNDERSTEERING: THE LOSS OF TRACTION ON THE FRONT TIRES

A vehicle understeers, or "pushes," when you turn the steering wheel and the vehicle doesn't turn as much as you've turned the steering wheel. In other words, the vehicle has a tendency to go in a straighter arc due to the front tires losing their grip. Entering a turn too fast and/or turning too late or too suddenly may cause understeer.

To correct understeer:
1. Gently let off the accelerator pedal. This transfers the weight toward the front of the vehicle, making the front contact patches bigger and providing more traction.

2. Once you're back on line, squeeze the accelerator.

3. Under extreme understeering conditions—when you've hit a curve way too fast or started your turn way too late—you may have to apply the brakes to transfer more weight to the front, but do it smoothly. If the front wheels lock up when braking, you will completely lose steering control and the vehicle will go straight or in whatever direction momentum carries it. Of course, if you've got ABS, that will help keep your wheels from locking up.

4. Note: If you're in four-wheel drive, you can apply more power to help power yourself out of an understeer situation. Give this a try, but only if you've got room to do it safely. For example, if you're deep into

>> You can power out of throttle oversteer if you've got four-wheel drive, but only apply the power if you've got plenty of room to do it safely. This goes for sand, snow, and other surfaces. *Ken Brubaker*

a corner and about to run off the road, then more brakes are probably better than more power.

Caution! All vehicles respond differently to letting off the accelerator pedal—especially depending on what gear you are in and if your 4WD system is engaged. Be aware of how your vehicle responds to this input. It may react very quickly to even minor corrections. Get familiar with your vehicle's "personality" so you know how it will react under a variety of conditions. Remember, practice makes perfect!

OVERSTEERING: LOSS OF TRACTION ON THE REAR TIRES

A vehicle oversteers (or is "loose") when, as you turn the steering wheel, the vehicle wants to turn even more. Eventually, the rear end of the vehicle will begin to slide out due to the rear tires losing traction. Oversteer may be caused by letting off the accelerator while turning or braking into a turn—especially if either are done too severely. Severe braking can cause the rear wheels to lock up. Remember, under heavy braking, the weight of the vehicle transfers to the front tires and the rear tires lift slightly and cause the contact patches to become smaller. With reduced traction in the rear, the vehicle can easily slide sideways and, if this is not corrected, the vehicle can spin.

To correct oversteer:
1. First and foremost, look at where you want to go.

2. Turn the steering wheel in the same direction as where the rear of the vehicle wants to go. This is called "counter steer," and the amount of counter steering is determined by where you point the front tires and aim the vehicle.

3. Next, gently press on the accelerator to transfer weight to the rear of the car. This is not done if the oversteer condition is caused by spinning rear tires. In that situation, see "Throttle Oversteer" in the next section.

4. As the rear end comes back in line, straighten out the steering wheel.

This approach works the same whether you're in a two-wheel- or four-wheel-drive vehicle. It is very easy to over-correct an oversteer condition, with the end result being that the vehicle will straighten out and then spin in the other way. Once you gain traction on all four tires, you will end up going where the front wheels are pointed. Therefore, always try to keep your front tires pointed in the direction you want the vehicle to travel.

THROTTLE OVERSTEER

Throttle oversteer is a condition caused by spinning the rear tires on a rear-wheel drive vehicle and is usually caused by giving too much throttle. Spinning tires have little or no traction and any steering input under this condition might cause oversteer. To correct this condition, ease off the throttle until the rear tires stop spinning while aiming the front tires where you want the vehicle to go. Again, if you're in four-wheel drive, you can correct oversteer by powering out of it. But, again, do so only if you've got room to safely do it.

NEUTRAL STEERING

Your ultimate goal is to keep your vehicle in a neutral steering condition at all times—that is, when your vehicle dynamics are in balance, with no understeer and no oversteer—so it does exactly what you want it to do. By having a basic understanding of understeer and oversteer, contact patches, and weight transfer you can balance your vehicle through proper use of the brake and accelerator pedal. Regardless of the corrections you make to maintain this balance, be smooth, and it will pay off.

Race car drivers have a tongue-in-cheek way of checking whether their vehicles are in an understeer, oversteer, or neutral condition: An understeering car goes off the track and through the fence nose first, an oversteering car goes off the track and through the fence tail first, and a neutral-steering car goes off the track and through the fence both ends at the same time.

Always remember: You and your vehicle have limits. With lots of practice and seat time, you can gradually raise your limits. Always stay within your limits as well as the limits of the vehicle.

Where is "the limit?" It's tough to teach a person where his or her limits are, and it's even harder to learn. Take small steps and you'll get there. Small mistakes mean small corrections. Big mistakes . . . well . . . try not to make big mistakes.

DRIVING IS THE
ULTIMATE ACT OF DISCIPLINE

Driving is a mental exercise. Your ability to perform your skills is very much dependent upon your state of mind. To properly manage your vehicle's systems, first you must be able to manage your own systems.

Anytime you can learn and understand the dynamics of a vehicle—why it acts a certain way under a particular set of circumstances—you'll be a better driver as a result. For example, understanding that when you put the brakes on hard, you take the weight off of the rear end and greatly increase your chances of a spinout. The more I raced and the more I thought about it, the more I realized that all I was doing was controlling four little tire patches. If I want to turn left, I've got to use my brakes to get the weight into the front end. I can't make a good left turn and be accelerating at the same time because I've got to get weight up front to make it turn.

PARNELLI JONES—MY HERO

Talk about a guy who knows what smooth driving is all about! Parnelli Jones was my hero as I worked my way up through the off-road driving ranks. Since then, I've gotten the chance to meet him and become friends. I remember things that happened with Parnelli over the years, and I smile. Parnelli told me he was once being interviewed by a journalist who asked him, "How can you tell the fast race cars from the slow race cars before a race?" They were walking around the contingency area where the race cars were all parked in one big lot before they raced the next day. Parnelli said to the journalist, "Oh, it's easy. The fast ones have a great big bumper on the front, and the slow ones have a big bumper on the back." I hadn't thought about it, but that is the truth because, in off-road racing, when you catch somebody on a dirt road, they have to get out of your way if they hear you, and then you go ahead and pass them. In Baja, it's not like you've got a two-lane road to work with. You're lucky that you've got one lane while, at the same time, they're making a big cloud of dust, and you're trying to get their attention to pass by honking your horn. Sometimes that's just not enough.

The unwritten rule in off-road racing is that you can honk to signal to someone in front of you that you want to pass, and if the driver doesn't get out of the way, you can give him or her a little bump. If the driver still

doesn't move over, you can give the vehicle a bigger bump. That's why you've got the big bumper—on the back if you're the guy who's always getting passed, and the front if you're the one doing the passing.

Somebody once asked Parnelli, "How do you pass all these people?" Parnelli said "Well, you honk and you bump—and [as he snapped his fingers] it happens about that quick." I always thought that was cool. Another journalist asked, "Parnelli, when you started, there were 270 cars on the road ahead of you, and by the halfway point, you had passed them all. How did you do that, and where'd you pass them?" Parnelli answered, "I just passed them where I caught them." To me, that was the coolest thing. He just passed the other cars where he caught them. That's all you can do. Whenever you catch them, you pass them. What people didn't know in those days was that probably a lot of those cars were broken down. The technology in those early days wasn't so great. Most of the off-road racers were driving four-banger VW-powered vehicles, and Parnelli had a big, V-8-powered Ford Bronco.

Parnelli was a real man's man. He raced everything—off road, Trans-Am, and the Indy 500. He punched Eddie Sachs in the nose at Indianapolis. He drove midgets, sprint cars, and much more. He's in his 70s now, but in his younger years he drove solo in the Baja 1000, and he soloed and won the Baja 500. That was one of the reasons I got into off-road racing. I figured if Jones could do it, then I could do it, too.

EMERGENCY BRAKING TECHNIQUES

If you are going fairly fast and see that you're about to hit a large hole, you should get on your brakes as hard as possible and as quickly as possible without locking them up or skidding. I know that's a tall order, but with practice you can improve both your emergency braking technique and your reaction times. Many off-road driving classes practice emergency braking techniques with obstacles in the driver's path that must be avoided at a relatively high rate of speed. Believe me, practice does make perfect when it comes to learning how to brake to avoid obstacles.

Just before you reach the hole, let off the brakes. This way your tires are going to roll through the hole with full suspension travel, which gives you much better odds that something won't break.

If your brakes are locked up, the weight of the vehicle transfers to the front wheels, effectively doubling the weight to the front end via the G-force and gravity. This also loads your suspension up and takes away the travel you have to absorb the impact with the hole. This also takes away the weight from the rear axle, and trucks and SUVs are lighter in the rear than a car. This can affect handling and bring the rear of your vehicle around in a fishtail motion, causing you to totally lose control of your vehicle.

BE READY . . . CONCENTRATE . . . FOCUS

KNOW THE BOTTOM OF YOUR VEHICLE

One thing that figures into whether or not you'll be able to negotiate certain off-road obstacles is your vehicle clearance—that is, the distance between the ground and low-hanging parts of your vehicle. These parts include your transmission, differentials (front and rear, depending on your vehicle's configuration), mufflers, exhaust pipes, suspension components, oil pans, and so forth. If your clearance is low, the kinds of off-road adventures you'll be able to experience will be limited to those that do not involve much in the way of obstacles such as rocks, logs, ruts, holes, and the like. If your clearance is high, your universe of possible off-road adventures will be much larger.

- Know the clearance under your differentials—front and rear—and their location under the vehicle. Some are offset to the right or left instead of in the center.

- Know the clearance of the lowest thing under your

>> **Know the bottom of your vehicle, or you may be in for a big surprise.** *Rick Shandley*

| CHAPTER 6: ADVANCED OFF-ROAD DRIVING SKILLS

vehicle. This could be the differential, tailpipe, tow hitch, spring shackle, and so forth. Know where your driveline is exposed.

- Have an idea of where your tires stand in relation to both the inside of the vehicle and with the hood line.

- Just in case a rock ends up some place it shouldn't be, it's a good idea to have some good skid plates installed underneath your vehicle. If you're buying a new car, truck, or SUV, many offer off-road option packages that include skid plates, or you may be able to buy them individually. There are also an amazing number of aftermarket skid plate options available for just about any vehicle you might consider taking off road.

No vehicle can get over every possible off-road obstacle out there. When in doubt, be sure you've got a plan for getting out if you get stuck—a winch or a buddy and a tow strap—or try to avoid the obstacle altogether. If you can't avoid it, and if you don't have a good plan for getting out of trouble, you should turn back.

DRIVING AT NIGHT

The idea of driving at night is challenging enough, but combine driving at night with driving off road and for many, this is a good reason for parking your rig and getting settled into your campsite, trailer, or cabin until morning. Unless you've absolutely got to keep moving, my personal advice is to avoid driving off road at night unless you've got the following aspects covered:

>> **Take a minute to check the clearance of the lowest thing under your vehicle—before you hit something, not after!** *Rick Shandley*

- You know the area—well. This is no time to be finding your way around unfamiliar territory. When it's dark, it's awfully hard to see what's on the other side of that little rise in the shadows in front of you. Is there a ditch—or a cliff—on the other side?

- You've got the right equipment. Your speed is limited by how far you can see. Additional lighting is recommended for any off-road night driving, but remember, when using auxiliary lighting, the vehicle's alternator must be able to provide enough amps to use all the candlepower. Make sure your electrical system is up to snuff. Also, some states restrict the use of off-road lighting on on-road vehicles, and for good reason. Some off-road lights can send a beam five miles or more. Imagine driving down the road and getting flashed by those! Know the rules about when you can and can't use off-road lights.

The less familiar you are with an area in which you're driving at night, the more important your equipment becomes. There are three basic kinds of lights to consider when you're going off-road:

Driving lights are a big step up from the stock lights that come in most vehicles. They are brighter and throw a beam of light farther, making for much safer driving.

Long-range lights are an even brighter, more powerful kind of driving light—we're talking miles here—that's particularly well suited for driving faster and for extreme off-road driving conditions.

Fog lights, on the other hand, push out a low, wide beam that's great to have when you find yourself in fog. The light won't bounce back into your eyes the way the beam from your regular lights will in fog, snow, or other bad weather conditions.

The general rule of thumb on lighting is to get as much as you need for your particular purpose. If you're driving at night, and you don't feel comfortable because you can't see very well or far enough ahead of your vehicle, that's a good indication that you need more lighting. The stock lights that came with your vehicle are probably just fine for occasional off-roading. If, however, you're seriously into the off-road adventure scene, loading up your rig with additional lighting equipment is a good idea. Many of the lighting manufacturers—PIAA, Hella, KC, and others—have equipment guides on their websites to help you decide which lights will work best for you. Be sure to check them out before you shell out a bunch of money for something that may be more than you need—or not enough.

When you encounter dark spots beware of them, since there is nothing to reflect the light back and distinguish what is hiding in the dark. When I used to race in Baja, not being able to see what was in the shadows was a real problem. When you'd see a group of people standing around, you'd know something was up. It was almost guaranteed that they had dug a hole or a big ditch to have some fun. One of the reasons we would prerun the race was to find these booby traps and keep notes on where they were. But the locals were smart, and they would dig new booby traps in the time between our prerun and the race.

One time coming out of Ensenada, we drove through a little community where some of the locals had dug a hole that had to be 15 feet wide and 6 feet deep. I remember hitting the berm in front of the hole, and I thought I was going to go over a cliff because the hole was so deep. It was like a tank trap. The guys who dug the booby trap were hiding in the bushes and I couldn't see them. I'm sure they all thought it was really funny.

Sometimes these little jokes were really dangerous. Out of San Felipe—just three miles from the start—some local guys built a booby trap in an area approaching Zoo Road, which is a 120-mile-per-hour road. They buried a couple of telephone poles in the ground to create a jump ramp in an area where you're going slightly uphill. When you're doing 120 miles per hour, you can't see the jump, and you're not ready for it. A couple of my guys hit the trap. Larry Ragland tore the right front end clean off his car. Another guy rolled his rig. They're lucky they didn't get killed.

>>**Skid plates are well worth their price for anyone considering participating in some serious off-road adventures.** *Rick Shandley*

... YOU'LL IMMEDIATELY NOTICE THAT SOMETHING

FEELS DIFFERENT.

chapter 7

DIRT
AND
DUST

If you've ever taken a car or truck off a paved road and onto a dirt road, you'll immediately notice that something feels different. The reason a dirt road feels different than a paved road is because it is different than a paved road. Paved roads are optimized for traction. Whether paved with asphalt or cement, rubber tires do a good job of sticking to it, even through turns and fast starts and stops. Dirt roads and trails, however, are not optimized for traction. In fact, slipping around as you gun the accelerator or hit the brakes or take a corner a bit faster than you should is the norm.

Driving in the dirt and dust is usually the first step in off-road driving, and it's a lot of fun even for the seasoned off-roader. For these reasons and more, learning how to deal with dirt is something every off-road adventurer needs to do.

DIRT: OFF-ROAD PLAYGROUND

When most of us think of going on an off-road adventure, getting off the pavement and onto a dirt road or trail immediately comes to mind. Driving in the dirt is the foundation of off-road driving and while it can be a challenge, it's also a lot of fun.

When driving in the dirt, the main thing to understand is that the driving dynamics are considerably different than driving on regular pavement. On pavement, you've got a fairly predictable surface that's not going to throw too many surprises at you, aside from the occasional pothole, torrential rain storm, blizzard, or sheet of black ice. On the other hand, dirt is a much less predictable surface. Dirt can be slippery, bumpy, hard, or soft, and you may encounter most any surface imaginable—flat roads, ruts, ditches, jumps, and anything else you could imagine.

So, when things start getting sporty in the dirt, what should you do? It's pretty simple and straightforward:

>> **Driving in the dirt—good clean fun!** *Rick Shandley*

- Slow down!

- Use a very steady, consistent pace.

- Keep the tires on the ground at all times.

- Avoid really deep ruts if possible. High centering can occur even on small obstacles when your tires are down low in ruts.

- Know where your differentials are in uneven terrain; also know where your tire placement is at and what direction your tires are heading.

- Try to outrun your dust cloud if it's interfering with your visibility.

As in many situations off road, lowering your speed will generally get you through more situations than raising it. Of course, there are always exceptions to this rule, such as trying to outrun a dust cloud or getting through a mud bog, so you've got to get familiar with which approach is best for your particular situation.

LIVING LA VIDA LOCA

A lot of people think that when you race in Mexico, they close down the roads. That's definitely never been the case in all the years I raced the Baja 500 and 1000, and it's definitely not the case today. While racing, there are pig farmers, school buses, cows, water trucks, and everyday people coming at you from the other direction all the time. You just learn to expect the unexpected. You can be driving along at 100 miles per hour when a

>> **Most off-road adventures start in the dirt—it's usually the first step for anyone who decides to see what happens when they take their rig off a paved road.** *Rick Shandley*

CHAPTER 7: DIRT AND DUST

horse—or a child—walks right out in front of you. I just don't know how I got to be as old as I am; I have had so many close calls.

The closest I have ever been to getting killed was during a Baja 500. I was chasing a guy on a road in the Valle Trinidad, doing maybe 80 or 90 miles per hour. I was in this guy's dust, and my visibility was low. The only way I was going to pass him was by getting up close to him, which meant hanging out in his dust until I could get past him. You may not like to get in that dust because you never know when a cow is going to pop up right in front of you, but if you don't get right in there and drive through it, you're never going to get around whoever's in your way. You'll end up following someone for 500 miles and never have a chance of winning.

Somewhere along the line, you've got to be brave enough to get up there in his dust cloud and bump him to let him know you're there. Chances are the other driver can't see you because of all the dust he's making.

Anyway, I was racing in the Valle Trinidad, and I was pulling up in this guy's dust cloud getting ready to pass. What I couldn't see is that there was a two-ton truck parked right out in the middle of the road. The guy in front of me wasn't stuck in a dust cloud like I was, so he could see the truck, but I couldn't. So I blasted through the dust at 80 or 90 miles an hour, and there must have been an angel looking out for me that day, because I missed plowing into that parked truck by just a couple of feet. I didn't see it until I was right up on it. And, as soon as I got past it, I started thinking about the poor

>> **Dust here, dust there—there's dust everywhere.** *Rick Shandley*

guys behind me in my dust cloud. Fortunately, nobody hit that truck. I couldn't believe it.

DUST: FRIEND OR FOE?

Dust can be the off-road racer's best friend. When you kick up a big cloud of dust as you're zipping along, drivers following close behind you can have one heck of a time seeing where they are going. Sometimes they'll have to slow down and, sometimes, just stop. It can get so bad that they can't see more than 5 or 10 feet in front of their hoods. But, when you're heading out for a casual off-road adventure with a friend, dust isn't the greatest thing to have around. Somebody's rig is going to get dirty, and someone's going to be eating a lot of dust along the way. It's not my idea of fun. I'd rather be making the dust than eating it.

Dust is a serious driving hazard you've got to deal with when it becomes a problem for you. Dust doesn't just have to be kicked up by someone else to be a problem. It can be the direct result of your own vehicle. Imagine that you're driving down the road and it's really, really dusty and silty. You're headed due east, you're doing 20 miles per hour, and the wind is blowing from your back at say 22 miles per hour. Guess what's going to happen? That big cloud of dust you're kicking up is going to catch up with and surround you. You aren't going fast enough to get out of your own dust, and that's a problem because your vision will be obscured and you'll soon be hacking and coughing from all that dust. What do you do? Try speeding up to outrun the cloud of dust. Once you get out of it, then there's a good chance you can stay out of it.

...DEALING WITH WATER CAN BE A

REAL CHALLENGE

chapter 8

>>WET
AND
WATER<<

Whether you're crossing a big puddle in the middle of a trail or trying to ford a stream or river, dealing with water can be a real challenge. First, wet roads and trails make for a loss of traction that translates into a loss of control. Second, when trying to cross a body of water, you usually can't tell how deep it really is, and it's hard to gauge the power of a fast-moving stream. Third, when you get out of the wet, your brakes are going to be a lot less efficient until they have a chance to dry out.

PREVIOUS PAGE >> **Water crossings are good fun in an off-road vehicle. Be sure and scout out the crossing before diving in with your truck. If the bottom is muddy, even a shallow crossing can be difficult to cross.** *Lee Klancher*

We deal with wet paved roads every time it rains, and we all know that they can sometimes be challenging to navigate. The harder it's raining and the faster we're going, the less traction we have at our disposal, and the more our vehicles want to start slipping. Now go off road and the potential loss of traction you'll experience in a 3-foot-deep moving stream of water. All of a sudden, we're talking a serious situation that takes planning and good technique to deal with.

CROSSING A WATER HAZARD

Crossing water hazards—especially large puddles or streams—can be one of the most exciting things you'll do during the course of your off-road driving adventures, but whether you're crossing just one water hazard or a series,

the idea is to make it exciting in a fun and safe way, not exciting in a terrifying and dangerous way. Here are some things to keep in mind as you approach a water hazard:

- Plowing full steam ahead into the water only works in the movies. Take it slow and steady.

- More often than not, the slower the water is running, the deeper it is. The deeper it is, the less chance you've got of getting through it safely.

- White water tells you that rocks are near the surface.

- Faster water usually indicates shallower depths.

- Choose an exit point first, your entry point second, and then plan your best route across. When you're selecting a good exit point, look for tracks on the other side of the water hazard left by other vehicles that would indicate previous successful crossings.

- If you can't judge the depth of the water crossing from the cab of your vehicle, get out and get your feet wet, use a stick, or throw a rock in to help choose your route across.

- In the water, rocks usually make better footing for your vehicle. Not only is the traction with your tires better, but also there's less chance you'll find yourself sinking into the soft, muddy bottom of the water hazard. If the bottom is hard, you know how deep the water is. If the bottom is soft, you really don't know the depth, so you may spin down and sink 12 inches or even deeper! Sand and gravel can suck your tires in and get your vehicle stuck. Let's not even talk about quicksand.

- Moving water creates extra force for your vehicle to overcome. This means selecting a lower gear, applying more power, and using constant steady movement. Use common sense and cross with—not against—the current.

- Always go slow when crossing water—just fast enough to maintain forward movement and to keep the current from pulling you downstream and away from your exit point.

>> Opposite page/Below: **Take it slow and steady when entering water, driving through it, and getting out. What's the hurry?** *Todd Horne*

- Going slow keeps splashing water from stalling your engine. You do not—repeat—you do not want your engine to stall when you're crossing a water hazard. Especially one that is moving quickly.

- The air cleaner can be temporarily waterproofed, if needed, by plugging the intake with rags and turning it toward the firewall.

- If you're going to get into some seriously deep water, consider disconnecting your fan belt (not your serpentine belts) to keep the fan from sucking water in through the radiator or blowing water onto your engine and electrics.

- After a deep or extremely long crossing has been exited, check your fluid levels—such as coolant, brakes, oil, and transmission—to see if they are abnormally high. If they are, that's a good indication that water got into the system and may need flushing and replacement.

Before you cross any water hazard, you should be aware of how deep your vehicle can go before it starts sucking water. You can generally get as deep as your hubs without problems, and maybe even up to the top of your tires, but before you find yourself out in the wilds facing that particular situation, know where your air intakes are and how high they are relative to the outside of your rig. If you're planning to do any serious deep-water crossings as a part of your off-road travel adventure, consider investing in an aftermarket snorkel system that will raise your air intake up above your windshield.

IT'S NOT ALWAYS FUN IN THE SUN

John Johnson, a buddy of mine, got stuck in a wash in Baja just out of Gonzaga Bay with a flash flood rushing toward him and his wife. The water was coming fast, his rig was stuck in the sand, and he was in a very bad situation. As the water got deeper and deeper, John knew that if he didn't think of something fast, he would lose his vehicle. He took a spare tire and somehow ran a rope across it, around his axle, and over to a big, dead tree so that as he drove forward, it lifted the back of his car up out of the sand. Little by little he was able to move forward and out of the fast-rising water. That was thinking fast!

Crossing a moving body of water is never something you should take for granted. In many cases, it's impossible to see just how deep the water is, and to judge if your vehicle will make it across. Lots of horrible things can happen, such as getting bogged down in the water, having your engine suck water into its air intake—bad news—or, if the water is moving quickly enough, seeing

your vehicle get washed downstream. Needless to say, all of these possibilities would ruin a perfectly good day.

The best thing you can do if you get washed down a river is to open both doors. Cars are buoyant when the doors are closed. They may not float, but there's very little weight on the tires. If you notice that happening, open the doors, and let the water in. That keeps the vehicle on the ground, and if the motor is still running and the water's not too deep, you can drive out. When you've got to cross a river, before you start across, think: "What's the worst thing that can happen? The very worst thing is that I'm going to start floating, and if I start floating, here's what I'm going to do." Again, engage your brain before you do something that you may regret!

>>**Sometimes you've just got to go with the flow.**

PAVED ROADS AREN'T ALL THEY'RE

chapter 9
>>PAVED ROADS<<

CRACKED UP TO BE.

Paved roads aren't all they're cracked up to be. Okay, sometimes they are cracked up—full of potholes, dips, and far worse. Because most off-road vehicles are designed differently than most normal on-road vehicles—higher centers of gravity and different tires—they don't handle the same way. If you're used to driving a regular car or truck, understand that an off-road vehicle or SUV with a higher center of gravity is going to handle differently—even on paved roads—and if your off-road vehicle starts handling differently on the road when you least expect it, you can quickly find yourself in a world of hurt.

OFF-ROAD VEHICLES ARE DIFFERENT

Even if you buy a stock SUV, the manufacturer will be sure to warn you that this particular kind of vehicle is different from a regular car or truck. In fact, you'll probably have to read three or four different warnings—plastered on your sun visor, hanging on your headrest, and printed all over your user's manual—before you get a chance to even pull out of your driveway.

The reason for all these warnings is because SUVs are different from regular vehicles. Most have a higher center of gravity than regular cars or trucks, which makes them "tippy" and prone to rolling in certain situations. The reason they have a higher center of gravity is because they are built with higher ground clearance to safely maneuver over off-road obstacles such as rocks and logs. Take a regular car and drive 30 miles an hour around a sharp curve, and in the worst case, it will spin out. Do the same thing in an SUV, and it can flip over and roll. If you've never seen a vehicle that has been through a rollover accident, let me tell you, it's not a pretty sight. Broken glass and crushed roofs are par for the course. As long as you don't get in too much of a hurry—or stop too quickly—chances are you'll never have a problem.

>> **Be careful—and look both ways—when crossing a paved road.** *Rick Shandley*

>> **Thompson Pass on the Richardson Highway in Alaska is one of the most beautiful stretches of pavement in America.** *Lee Klancher*

Of course, there are a few other things that can happen on road in a vehicle that's designed for off-road use. The tires are bigger, and they may be designed to run both on road and off road. This means the tire manufacturer has made a compromise, and the tires won't handle as well on paved roads as normal street tires would. Cornering, braking, and acceleration are all going to be compromised, too.

Be alert to how your off-road vehicle handles on road, and factor that into your decision making when you approach a corner, tackle a wet patch of road, or have to make a panic stop.

Here are a few other tips to keep in mind as you drive on paved roads:

>> below and opposite: **Even stock SUVs are different than cars and trucks. They have a higher center of gravity so it's important to be aware of your surroundings, and the limits of your vehicle. No matter what you choose, all can be fun on a paved road.**

- Stay within the speed limit. Too many accidents are the result of people driving faster than their vehicles or the conditions allow.

- Wear your seat belt. If you do lose control and crash, you'll have a much better chance of surviving if you wear your seatbelt.

- Drive defensively. Always assume the other driver is going to do something that will put you in danger, and be prepared to take action accordingly.

- Take your time. Mistakes happen when you're in a hurry. What's the rush?

- Keep an eye on your blind spots. Few rearview mirrors provide complete coverage of the panorama behind your vehicle. Make a point of seeking out your vehicle's blind spots and periodically checking to see if anyone is in them.

THE BRUCE JENNER INCIDENT

Back in 1983 or thereabouts, I signed up to run the Las Vegas to Reno race with the 1976 Olympic decathlon winner, Bruce Jenner. During that period of time I was driving in off-road races for Ford, and Bruce was also driving for Ford in road races. I got a call from Ford wanting to know if I would take Bruce Jenner as my co-driver on this Las Vegas to Reno race. I said, "Sure," and the deal was done.

Before the race, I decided it would be a good idea to take Bruce along with me when I preran the race. We were about halfway between Las Vegas and Reno when I got too close to a guide marker on the side of the highway and hit it. BAM! It blew the mirror off of Bruce's side of the truck, which scared him and scared me, too. After we had a chance to calm down, Bruce said, "Ivan, you've got to remember now that if you kill me, your claim to fame is going to be you are the guy who killed the famous Bruce Jenner."

I thought about that for a minute and said, "Yeah, you're probably right. That wouldn't look too good on my resume." And it was true. The last thing I wanted to be was the racer who killed Bruce Jenner—the guy who was on the front of every Wheaties box from here to New York City.

>> **Next Page: Some stretches of pavement are remote enough to be worth the effort. This pristine piece of blacktop is part of Alaska's Dalton Highway, which runs 400 miles north of Fairbanks to Prudhoe Bay. The highway is the farthest north you can drive in North America, and this shot was taken more than 100 miles north of the Arctic Circle on an unusually warm day in July 2005.** *Lee Klancher*

>> **The road through Estes Park in Colorado is another beautiful stretch of road worth taking your ORV on pavement to see. Note that this stretch is best seen mid-week and early in the day, as it gets crowded in the summer.** *Lee Klancher*

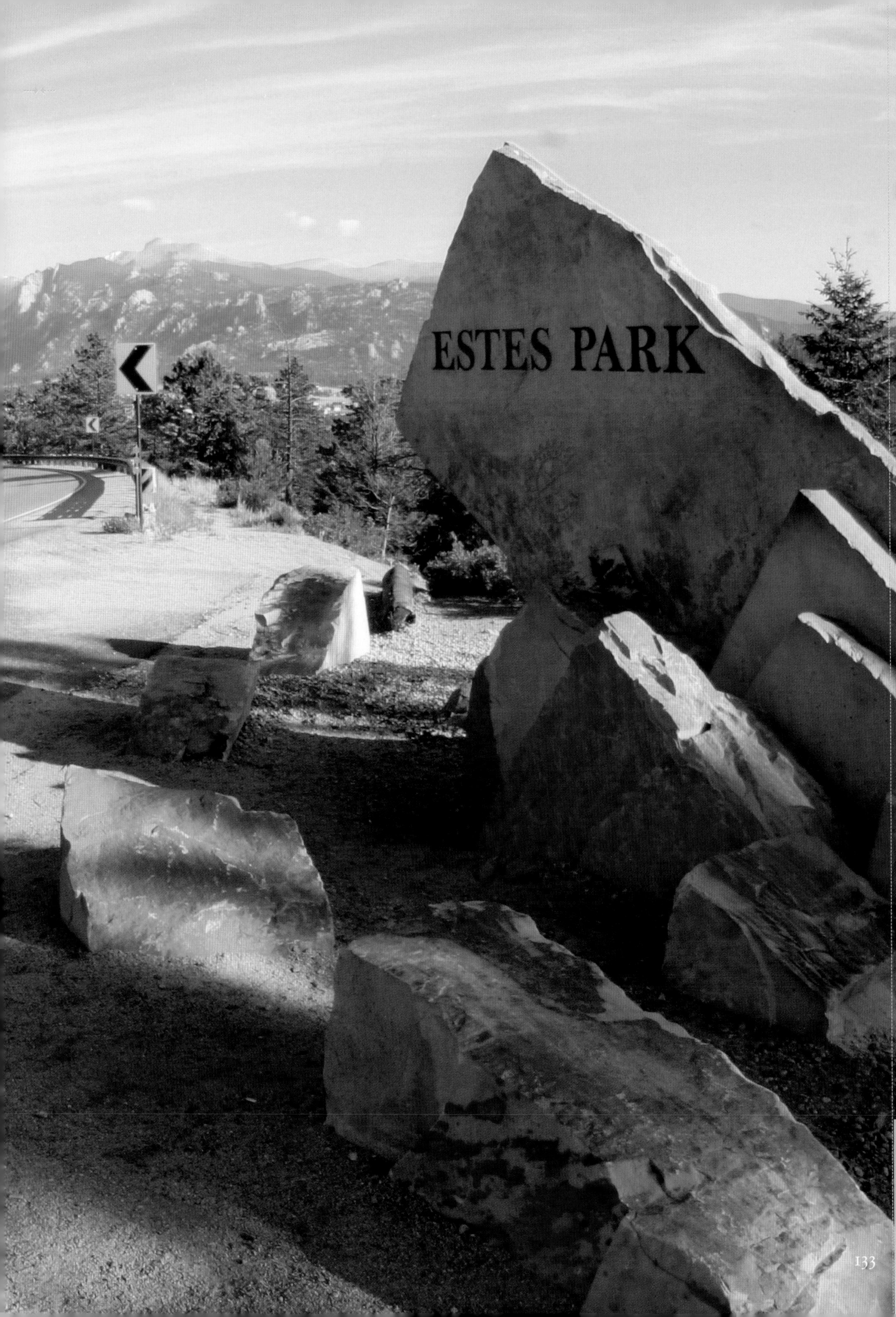
ESTES PARK

OFF-ROADING IN SAND OFFERS A UNIQUE

DRIVING CHALLENGE

chapter 10

>>SAND<<

Whether you're driving through a short patch of sand on an otherwise hard-packed trail, or driving on a beach along the ocean, or blasting your way up or down a huge sand dune out in the middle of the desert, off-roading in sand offers a unique driving challenge. In some cases, letting some air out of your tires—front and rear—will be all you need to do to keep moving. In other cases, you might need to do something more. In this chapter, I explain how to keep your vehicle moving forward and avoid getting stuck when driving through sand—and how to get unstuck when you do.

GETTING THROUGH THE SAND

Believe it or not, you don't have to have a four-wheel drive vehicle to drive through the sand. While it's definitely a good idea to have four-wheel drive for most informal off-road travel adventures (such as the ones I take when I go on my own adventures with friends and family), I should point out that our current Baja Protruck racers are all two-wheel drive. In fact, just to be sure, we did a lot of testing in some pretty big sand dunes with our Baja Protrucks. The driver can deflate his tires to get the great big footprint he needs to get through the sand. When he gets to the other side of the dunes, he can fill the tires right back up again. By deflating your tires, you can really improve your vehicle's performance in the sand whether your vehicle is two- or four-wheel drive.

In 1995, Toyota asked me to go out to Borrego, which is a large desert park east of San Diego, to be part of a media ride and drive for the launch of the new Land Cruiser SUV and Tacoma pickup truck. This is where Toyota offered members of the automotive press a chance to test out these new vehicles for themselves in some challenging terrain. One of the journalists had taken a truck up one of the off-road sections and slid down a sandy hill, putting the vehicle in a sideways position just down from the crest of a hill. He had tried to back the truck down, but he couldn't get it in the right position, and the vehicle was almost ready to roll over.

The reporter understandably wanted to get out—quick—and turn his rig over to the professional drivers who were there to help out, but he was buckled into his seat belt and tilted so far over that his seat belt wouldn't unlatch. So, his vehicle was stuck, his seat belt was stuck, and his vehicle was just about to go over. I was certain that the rig was going to start tumbling down the hill. To make a long

>> **Select your route to float on top of the sand instead of digging in.** *Rick Shandley*

story short, I got up, leaned into the cab of the truck, and managed to get his belt loose. We were then able to get the vehicle down off the hill. That was a close one, and a good example of the kind of thing that can happen when you're on a sandy hill and start slipping sideways.

Sand can be found just about anywhere, so while you might not be planning to find any sand during the course of your off-road travel adventure, it might just be planning to find you. Here's what to do when you meet up with more than just a little bit of sand:

- Stop to evaluate the situation and plan your route.

- Select the route by reading the terrain. Look for spots with rocks, plants, sticks, or other debris that might help you "float" above the sand and offer better traction.

>> **Don't forget that letting air out of your tires can make a big difference when you're trying to get through a serious patch of sand.**
Rick Shandley

- Consider decreasing the air pressure in your tires, but be sure to re-fill them to the correct pressure as soon as you've driven through the sand hazard. Again, creating a larger tire patch will help you float on top of the sand rather than digging into it.

- Choose a gear that will allow enough speed to get through the sand without having to shift up or down. Tire slippage creates a loss of traction and slows your momentum.

- Keep a steady throttle. Let the weight of the vehicle work for you.

- Optimize your use of power and speed so you won't have to shift up or down.

- Once you get going, try not to stop until you've made it through to the other side. On sand, it's important to get some momentum going, and then keep it going.

- If you've got a large patch of sand to tackle, and your traction is not the best, consider driving through it at night or in the early morning when the sand is damp and traction is better.

ENGAGE BRAIN FIRST, THEN GO

One time we were doing a TV commercial for Toyota at El Mirage Dry Lake. Thousands of automobile commercials have been filmed there over the years. One of the crew members who was helping with the commercial warned us to watch out for this particular director. Apparently, at the end of the day of filming, the director would get people so worked up that somebody would inevitably get hurt. I thanked the crew member for the warning, but I didn't think much about it.

We were up at El Mirage for two or three days working on this TV commercial. The production crew had two race trucks used for filming that were identical in appearance to use for the filming. The whole gist of the commercial was, as I whistle, my truck comes to me like a dog would when you whistle for him to come. This was actually a pretty good trick because the way they filmed it, it looked like there was no one driving the truck. They made it appear as if I just whistled and the truck came all by itself.

Of course, there was no magic to how we pulled off this

feat. They took the seat out of one of the trucks and put my son Brian in the truck to drive it. He could crouch down so the camera couldn't see him driving, but the camera could see me and the truck coming toward me. So we started filming. I whistled, and the truck would come, but it kept veering out of the picture. Brian couldn't stick his head up to see where he was driving, so steering was a tough assignment. The director would tell him, "Turn right—a little more, a little more." Eventually we got the shot and wrapped it up.

At least I thought we wrapped it up. The next day the director decided he wanted to get a few more shots for the commercial. Finally, the sun was setting and we were almost done. They have different names in the movie business for the two trucks we were using to film the commercial. One truck was called the "hero" because it was the beautiful, shiny one that was kept clean as a whistle all the time. The other truck (the one without the seat) was called the "mule," the one that didn't have a seat in it, which we mainly used for my whistle shot.

So it was the end of the second day, and all the producers, sound people, makeup people, and the camera guys were getting ready to pack it up and head back home. Well, not quite. The director suddenly said, "Oh, that sunset is gorgeous! Ivan, is there any chance you could get in that other truck over there real quick before the sun sets and just slide it in front of the camera?" The other truck over there was the mule, and the mule didn't have a seat. I'd already forgotten about the warning I'd gotten from the crew member, and volunteered, "Yeah, I suppose I can."

So the director's in a big hurry because the sun is setting and he's going to lose his shot. I pointed out that the truck he wanted to use didn't have a seat in it, and he said "Oh,

>> **Once you get going through the sand, don't stop until you get to the other side!** *Rick Shandley*

that's a shame because there's going to be a beautiful sunset and it would be perfect for the commercial." The writing was on the wall, and I jumped in the truck. Well, not only did it not have a seat but, without a seat, you can't put the seat belts on. So the director tells me, "The camera is over here, and we want you to come in from over there and slide in the sand around this way. We'll just get the back of the truck and the spinning tires as you zoom off. Now, hurry, the sun's going to be gone soon!"

I ran through the shot once or twice and thought I did a good job, but the director said, "Let's get one more, the light is perfect right now." So, I drove over to my spot and swung the tail around. As the tail started sliding, the truck suddenly got up on two wheels. Getting up on two wheels wouldn't have been a big deal if it had been the two wheels on the driver's side because I would have been pushed against the door and been fine. But the truck got up on the two wheels on the passenger side. I didn't have a seat, I didn't have seat belts, and I didn't have the door to lean against. So I started falling toward the passenger door, my hands were coming off the steering wheel, and I was all screwed up and couldn't catch the truck.

Sure enough, it started tumbling, and I was rolling in the truck. Now, I have rolled lots and lots of vehicles over the years, but that was the only one I have ever rolled without a seat belt. Luckily I didn't go through the windshield because there wasn't any windshield. The film production guys had taken it out so it wouldn't cause reflections in the commercial. I banged my knee pretty bad on the shifter, but that was the extent of my injuries. I couldn't believe I had done that—the kind of rookie mistake that a seasoned vet like me should never make. I could have easily been killed because the director was in a rush, and I didn't step back and say, "Slow down."

>> **There are lots of off-road areas where you can practice driving through the sand. Some states will even let you drive your rig on the beach (check your local laws first, though).** *Rick Shandley*

... ITS NOTHING SHORT OF A MESS

chapter 11

>>SILT<<

Silt is a special kind of off-road condition that deserves its own chapter. You'll mostly run into silt in dry lake beds that have seen lots of off-road vehicle traffic, and it's nothing short of a mess. Silt is dry and fine, much like talcum powder. It gets into everything—your eyes, nose, and lungs, and your vehicle's air intake, engine, clutch, and more. Not only that, but because you can't see what's underneath the silt layer, you can be unpleasantly surprised when you hit a big rock, deep hole, or rut that grabs your tires and gets you stuck fast.

Silt is the result of the mechanical weathering of rocks by glaciers, rain, and wind, and by rivers and streams. Silt is not the same thing as sand, clay, or dirt, and it acts differently when you drive in it. That's probably why it's earned the nicknames "stone dust" and "rock flour." Whatever you do, just don't use it to bake a cake.

ALL ABOUT SILT

If you're driving off road, you'll often find silt in or around dry lakes, or in the bottom of streams and rivers. It is a type of soil that typically doesn't have rocks, sand, or gravel in it, but when it rains, it gets hard. When it's dry, and when a vehicle drives through it and stirs it up, it acts so much like a liquid that you can see waves move along the surface like you're in a boat on a lake. It's almost like quicksand without the water. Until you've actually been in silt and gotten stuck in it and had it down your clothes, in your eyes, and in your carburetor, it's a hard thing to describe and understand.

Wet silt in a river bed acts pretty much like mud. Driving through dry silt isn't particularly difficult, but the big problem with silt is that it goes everywhere and gets into everything. You and your rig will know when you've been running in silt because you both will be wearing it, breathing it, and eating it. The biggest problem with silt is, as lots of vehicles go over a particular spot in the road, it gets dug down and eventually becomes a rut you can't see under the silt—actually two ruts, one for each side of your vehicle. That makes it hard to tell where the good road ends and where the bad road begins, and it makes it hard to tell how deep the rut is. This opens up the very real possibility that you'll get stuck because the rut is deeper than you thought. Plus, in the center, there's no silt, just hard dirt. So, you get high bottomed on the hard center, and your tires just spin helplessly with nothing to grab on to.

DRIVING THROUGH SILT

Silt is a special condition—not quite like sand, not quite like dirt, and not quite like mud. It's really got its own thing going. For most off-road adventurers, the best plan is to get through it as quickly as possible. Here are some tips for doing just that:

- Before driving onto the surface of a dry lake, check for soft mud that may ring the lake and cause you to bog down.

- Consider wearing goggles to keep powdery silt from getting into your eyes and temporarily impairing your vision.

- Don't stop! Get to firm ground as soon as you can.

- Keep a steady throttle. Let the weight of the vehicle work for you.

- Choose a gear that will allow enough speed to get through the silt without having to shift up or down. Tire slippage creates a loss of traction and slows your momentum.

While there are no specific modifications you should make to your rig to get through silt, I highly suggest that you set your climate control system to "recirculate" and close any vents and windows so you don't suck too much of the stuff into your driving compartment. Also, silt—especially the kind you'll find on and around desert lake beds—can be very corrosive, so be sure to hose off your rig as soon as you can after you get out of it. They don't call them alkali dry lake beds for nothing!

WHY I'M NOT A BIG FAN OF SILT

I don't like driving in fog, and I don't know anybody who does. Silt acts a lot like fog. Driving through silt takes a lot of power because it bogs the engine down, and you have to really stand on the gas to keep moving forward. Of course, when you've got your throttle pushed hard, the butterfly in your carburetor is open and it's sucking the silt right into your engine.

I learned a trick years ago racing through silt. The trick is to go slow enough to keep the guy behind you from passing you while letting the guy in front of you get far enough away so you can see where you are going. Never change gears while you're driving through silt because it will end up getting into your clutch—hazing the clutch plates and making a real mess. Pick a gear and leave it there.

When my wife, Linda, and I went on our first trip to Baja, we had a couple of Baja bugs and an old VW Squareback. A friend of ours had a Corvair. We got to Lake Chapala—one of the dry lakes you had to drive across back in those days—and it was really silty. We figured we would have no problem with that. Here we were with hopped-up vehicles and our big old tires. We were macho Americans, and we were going to just power right through that silt.

All three of us got stuck. And, since we were all stuck, there was no one left to pull us out. We really didn't know what we were going to do.

All of a sudden, here comes a local guy in a beat-up 1951 Chevy. He had bald tires, and if he was running on four of his six cylinders, I would have been surprised. Instead of trying to motor through the silt like we did, he was driving through the brush. I will never forget seeing his taillights as his car putt-putted off into the distance while we were all stuck up to our axles in silt.

>> **Where there's silt, there's fine, gritty, dust all over the place. And a big cloud of fine, gritty dust can ruin your day if you let it.**

... IT WOULDNT BE A REAL ADVENTURE WITHOUT A

5NMR849

moving forward ▷

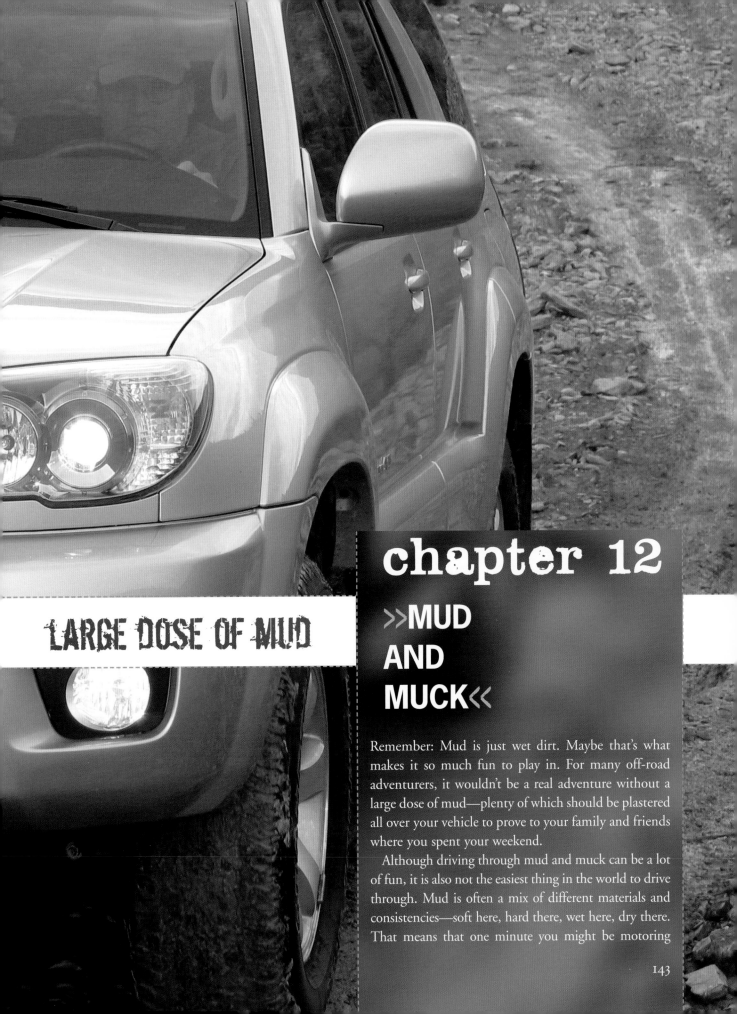

LARGE DOSE OF MUD

chapter 12

>>MUD AND MUCK<<

Remember: Mud is just wet dirt. Maybe that's what makes it so much fun to play in. For many off-road adventurers, it wouldn't be a real adventure without a large dose of mud—plenty of which should be plastered all over your vehicle to prove to your family and friends where you spent your weekend.

Although driving through mud and muck can be a lot of fun, it is also not the easiest thing in the world to drive through. Mud is often a mix of different materials and consistencies—soft here, hard there, wet here, dry there. That means that one minute you might be motoring along just fine through a mud hole, and all of a sudden you hit a rut that pulls your steering wheel out of your hands and launches your vehicle out of control. Or you hit a soft spot that sinks your rig right up to its axles—or deeper—and gets you so stuck that only help from a winch or another vehicle and a tow strap can get you out.

DRIVING THROUGH MUD

As is true with most obstacles, my first choice when encountering a muddy patch or puddle is to avoid it and drive around it if possible. However, when that's not possible, you've got to either forge ahead or retreat. How do you decide whether to go forward or go back? The first thing to consider is your tires. If you've got regular street tires, that's one strike against

you. You should invest in a good set of mud-terrain tires before you take on any serious mud. For most people, radial mud treads are the way to go because they work well in mud and are quiet on regular highways. They also work well in snow and on rocks. Just don't take them out in the rain or on ice. Slipping and sliding are their middle names in those conditions. Bias-ply mud treads are also an option, but they are very noisy and ride rough on regular roads. Any kind of mud tire will wear more quickly than a regular tire because they are generally made of softer rubber than regular street tires.

The second thing to consider is the size and depth of the muddy patch or puddle. Anything too far across and too deep will be another big strike against you. If you've

>> **Keep a steady throttle as you travel up a muddy trail.** *Rick Shandley*

got miles and miles of mud to deal with, you might want to rethink your route. Similarly, if the mud hole is too deep, and your differentials turn into mud plows, that's a sure sign you should consider a different route or turning around altogether. Get out of your vehicle and use a stick or shovel to measure just how deep that mud hole is. Can you feel the bottom? If not, turning back is probably the best decision you'll make all day.

Finally, do you have locking differentials? If not, that might just be the final strike. To keep your wheels from spinning uselessly, you'll need lockers to keep everything moving ahead. Be sure to lock your differentials before you hit the mud. They aren't going to do you much good if you've already gotten yourself stuck.

Aside from those things to think about before you hit the mud, here are some things to do when you do dive in.

- If you can drive around a big patch of mud instead of driving through it, do so.

- If you've chosen to drive through the mud instead of around it, keep a steady throttle. Let the weight of the vehicle work for you, and keep moving forward at a constant rate of speed.

- Keep an eye out for areas of firm ground—often to the sides of the mud patch—and try to get at least a couple of your wheels on them to provide more traction.

- Choose a gear that will allow enough speed to get through the mud hole without having to shift up or down. Tire slippage creates a loss of traction and slows your momentum.

>> Left: **When you're getting ready to do some serious mudding, you may want to bring along a rig that's built for the purpose.** Right: **Even stock vehicles can handle their share of mud and muck.** *Ken Brubaker*

>>ANSWERING THE CALL OF NATURE<<

I give a lot of talks about off-road racing and what it's like to participate in the Baja 500 and 1000. Every time I give one of these talks, someone wants to know the answer to this question: "What do you do when you have to go to the bathroom?"

Years ago, when you needed to answer the call of nature during a race, you had to make a choice. You could either pull over to the side of the road, stop your vehicle, take off your shoulder harnesses, get unbuckled, get out of your rig, and go behind a tree and do your thing while four or five vehicles zoomed by, leaving you behind, or you could just wet your pants. Nobody enjoyed that second option, but if it made the difference between winning first place or losing, you peed your pants instead of stopping your rig and taking time out of the race to take care of your business. That was one of the reasons I drove solo—I didn't like sitting in somebody else's pee.

Fortunately, somebody came up with this thing called an external catheter—the same thing the astronauts use in space. When the catheter is installed properly, you have a long hose running down your leg—and under your pants—taped in place so it won't move around. The hose comes out of the bottom of your pants and outside of your shoe. When you have to go to the bathroom, you just go—everything goes through the hose and into the foot well of your rig, which has holes drilled through to let water and other liquids drain out of the vehicle.

When you first put on this contraption you're supposed to trim off the hose—you don't want to drag it on the ground and look like a dork, and you don't want someone stepping on it. I once saw a cat chasing one guy's catheter. The experienced guys like me will trim it off and put it in our shoe before the race. As soon as you get into your vehicle for the race, you pull it out of your shoe and hit the road. At least, that was what you were supposed to do. I was racing the Parker 400, and I forgot to pull the catheter hose out of my shoe. Every time I peed, it went right into my shoe.

The cool thing about having a catheter on is that few people besides us racers know that we use them. When I was racing the Parker 400 again a few years later, I went into the restroom in the start area. There wasn't anyone around, so I put my foot up on the urinal, took the catheter hose out of my shoe, put it into the urinal, and did my business. Two guys walked in and saw me with my foot up on the urinal with a big river of pee pouring in. They looked at me—not saying a word—and I just stood there. I finished up, took my foot off the urinal, and started walking out of the bathroom. As I was leaving, I could hear one guy say to the other, "That's why they call that guy the Ironman!"

- Avoid spinning your tires. It might look cool with mud flying everywhere, but you'll lose traction, dig a hole in the mud, stop moving, and get stuck.

- If you find yourself with insufficient traction, let some air out of your tires to provide them with a larger surface area. Be sure to reinflate them after you get out of the mud.

- Bring along a tow strap, a shovel, and a winch if you're expecting to encounter serious mud, and know how to use them. It doesn't take all that much mud to get even the most experienced off-roaders stuck. Assume you're going to get stuck in the mud, and be prepared in the event you do.

>> **Mud + Snow = Slippery mess.** *Rick Shandley*

>> **Serious mudders use rigs specially modified to make the most of this slippery environment.** *Ken Brubaker*

... THE BOULDER WILL WIN ALMOST

EVERY TIME

chapter 13

>>ROCKS AND BOULDERS<<

From pebble gravel to giant boulders—and everything in between—most every off-road adventure offers some sort of encounter with rocks. While most encounters with rocks shouldn't cause you much problem, just one close encounter between a sharp rock and the sidewall of your tire can ruin a great day.

There's a difference between a rock and a boulder. First, let me say that you want nothing to do with hitting a boulder. Boulders are big, and they're hard, and in a contest between your rig and the boulder, the boulder will win almost every time. In the case of a boulder, winning means, at minimum, you're going to lose some paint, but in a worst-case scenario, you're going to bend your rig or break something and get stopped dead in your tracks.

Rocks, on the other hand, are a lot smaller, and although they're made out of the same stuff as boulders, you can reason with them. You can often simply drive around them. In fact, I advise that when you've got the option of driving over a rock or going around it, just go around it. Why invite problems when you don't have to? You'll have plenty of other opportunities to scramble over rocks when you have no other option but to do just that.

When you are forced to drive over a rock, hit it with the face of your tire, not on the sidewall. Your tire tread is designed to take the shock of hitting a rock or other obstacles. That's where all the fiberglass or steel belts are, but your sidewall is not designed to hit rocks. The sidewall is much thinner than the tread and does not have all the belts to protect it and it will puncture or tear fairly easily.

DRIVING THROUGH ROCKS AND BOULDERS

When faced with negotiating a rocky area, one of the most important things to keep in mind is ground clearance—the distance between the ground and low-hanging parts of your vehicle. We talked about this already in chapter 6, but I'm going to repeat it again here because it is so important. The low-hanging parts of your vehicle include your transmission, differentials (front and rear, depending on your vehicle's configuration), mufflers, exhaust pipes, suspension components, oil pans, and more. You should know exactly where these components are before you start working your way over the rocky stuff.

- Know the clearance under your differentials—front and rear—and their location under the vehicle. Some are offset to the right or left instead of in the center.

- Know the clearance of the lowest thing under your vehicle. This could be the differential, tailpipe, tow

>> **Make sure you know where those rocks are before you drive over them, not after!** *Rick Shandley*

>> **Sometimes your best approach is to drive your tires right over a rock—especially when straddling it might expose your differential and other low-hanging parts to damage.** *Rick Shandley*

hitch, spring shackle, and so forth. Know where your driveline is exposed.

- Have an idea of where your tires stand in relation to both the inside of the vehicle and with the hood line.

- Just in case a rock ends up some place it shouldn't be, it's a good idea to have some good skid plates installed underneath your vehicle. If you're buying a new car, truck, or SUV, many offer off-road option packages that include skid plates, or you may be able to buy them individually. There are also an amazing number of aftermarket skid plate options available for just about any vehicle you might consider taking off road.

No vehicle can get over every possible off-road obstacle out there. When in doubt whether or not yours will be able to make it, your first option should always be to turn back. That may be hard on your ego, but believe me, the bruises to your ego will heal a lot faster than the bruises to your rig or to your body that may result from forging on and getting in too deep. If you do decide to go forward, be sure you've got a plan for getting out if you get stuck—a winch or a buddy and a tow strap will come in handy here. Okay, now that we've got all the warnings out of the way, here are some tips for making your way through your everyday, garden-variety rocks:

- Before you start, look as far ahead as you reasonably can, and pick out a route that will allow you to avoid as many obstacles as possible, while putting you in good positions for the obstacles you can't avoid.

>> **When driving through rocks, protect your sidewall—it's weaker than the rest of your tire and can be easily damaged.** *Rick Shandley*

- Slow it down! It's your job to protect your tires and your drivetrain from the rocks that are just itching to leave a deep impression on them.

- Keep the vehicle in as straight a line as possible.

- Hit rocks straight on with your tire tread face. Avoid hitting your tire sidewalls.

- Instead of straddling rocks and potentially hitting something vital underneath your rig, drive on them with either your right or left tires depending on the clearance available. You've got to be very aware of your tire placement when you're driving through and over rocks. Pick a path for your tires, then follow it.

- Remember that solid rock provides good traction. Use it.

- Identify what rock is solid and what will slip or spit out from under the tires.

- If you're driving over or through larger boulders and can't see exactly where you are going, have your passenger jump out of the rig and act as a spotter to help guide you through.

If you think you're going to encounter lots of rocks during the course of your off-road adventure, I strongly suggest you beef up your tires before you go. First of all, the regular passenger car tires that come stock on most vehicles just aren't up to the task of crawling up, over, and around rocks and boulders. Get light truck tires that are built tougher to start with. Mud-terrain and aggressive all-terrain tires are a good choice because the rough tread grips rocky surfaces better than regular tires do. Yokohamas are my personal favorite, and they have long been popular with racers. Second, be sure that you get tires with at least three-ply sidewalls. When you're in the rocks, it's easy for one to tear through the side of your tire. Stronger sidewalls will help keep your tire together and you on your way.

MORE ON BOOBY TRAPS, JUMPS, AND OTHER OBSTACLES

When you first start racing, especially in Mexico, you have to think about why certain spectators are doing what they do. When a rookie racer sees a group of people standing around a particular spot, he thinks that the photographers are there because they want to get a great shot. "It's going to be spectacular because I'm going to race up there and make my vehicle jump like they've never seen before!" What the new racer soon learns, however, is that the reason everyone is standing around is because someone has put a log across the road, and they are looking to spice things up. In the afternoon of a race, it gets worse because the locals have been there watching this race all day long. A car might go by about every five or ten minutes, and the spectators are starting to get really bored.

The farther south you are and the farther into the race, the less often the vehicles come by, so spectators will throw a boulder out there—or a telephone pole or a little kid—just to make things exciting. I have a ton of friends in Mexico, so I never had that much trouble. I have hit some things that really woke me up, especially down around San Felipe, but I was really fortunate because I'd run in so many different races over the years that many of the locals knew me. If I got stuck, I had 100 locals who were going to push me out. So, having credibility and being around for a long time really pays off sometimes, but you still had to watch out for the booby traps, and you still do today.

Like anything else, some areas are worse than others. For example, the start of a race is a time to be particularly cautious. One time I was coming out of Mike's Sky Ranch going to Valle Trinidad. I was on a really narrow road, and it was 2 o'clock in the morning. I was going 90 to 100 miles per hour down this tight little dirt road, and I could see something in the middle of the road out in front of me. It looked like maybe a big boulder or a bush or something. When I got up to the object, I slowed down a little bit to go around it. It turned out to be a guy sitting in the middle of the road with his back to the race traffic. I could see his buddies out of the corner of my eye, and they probably dared him to see how long he would sit there, but what he didn't realize was that I could see him. When I turned all the lights on in my truck, it was like daylight out there.

I've seen guys along the course build little jumps—not very high, maybe as high as a chair—and they will dare each other to lay on the other side, thinking that racers will jump right over, but much to their surprise, some racers don't jump. In my case, since I usually didn't know what was on the other side—could be a log or anything—I would slow down and then drive across. Although I've never run over anyone, these accidents have happened to others in the past, and they will happen again in the future.

PLOTTING A COURSE

It's always a good idea to pick out a clear route through or around rocks and boulders before you find yourself in the middle of them with nowhere to go.

Remember Rock and Boulder Rule No. 1: It's always best to avoid them whenever possible. But if that's just not in the cards, be sure you use the faces of your tires to work your way over. In addition:

- Select your route by reading the terrain.

- Evaluate the use of power and speed.

- Select 2WD or 4WD, and select high or low 4WD.

- Plan your route.

- Evaluate your tire placement and vehicle clearances to avoid high centering or smacking anything under the vehicle.

- Maintain steady power for maximum traction.

- Keep alert for hidden obstacles under the rocks or inside the holes you're driving over.

- Constantly scan ahead toward your exit point.

>> **Rock crawling can be a lot of fun if you've got the right kind of rig. Kids: Don't try this at home!**

... MAKE WINTERTIME OFF-ROAD ADVENTURES

A REALITY

chapter 14

>>SNOW
AND
ICE<<

If you live where the temperature falls below freezing in the winter, you've probably already spent plenty of time driving a vehicle on snow-covered and ice-slicked roads. Having a four-wheel drive vehicle is a big plus when it comes to driving on snow and ice, and it can make wintertime off-road adventures a reality. But keeping out of trouble when driving through ice and snow is definitely a challenge.

Like mud and muck, driving through snow can be a lot of fun. Most off-road vehicles are up to the challenge, but you'll have to be extra careful to ensure that you don't end up in a ditch on the side of the road or caught in an uncontrollable slide when you hit a big patch of ice. There's a right way and a wrong way to drive on snow and ice. Let's consider the right way.

DRIVING THROUGH AND OVER THE WHITE STUFF

Whether you're on road or off road, driving through snow and ice can present a special challenge. Not only is the white stuff slippery, but if you break down, it's going to be cold—maybe very cold—outside your vehicle. You may be in danger from exposure to the elements. That said, it is particularly important to be prepared when you venture off road in the snow and ice. Check weath-

er conditions before you leave, and be alert to possible road closures. You should be sure your vehicle is in good health, and you should bring with you anything you might need to survive hours—or even days and nights—stuck in the snow and ice with no heater.

In addition, keep these driving tips in mind:

- Keep your speed down and use low gears to maintain traction on slippery surfaces.

- Unpacked or new snow will generally offer you better traction than snow that has been packed down by other travelers and that has gotten icy. Seek out unpacked snow whenever possible.

>> **There's nothing like fresh powder!** *Rick Shandley*

- Brake smoothly and gently to avoid causing your wheels to lock up. If you have ABS, do not pump your brakes!

- Give yourself plenty of room to brake between obstacles or a vehicle ahead of you.

- If your brakes do lock up and your rear wheels start to skid, take your foot off the accelerator and steer your vehicle in the direction you want your front wheels to go. For example, if your rear wheels start sliding to the left, then steer left. Be prepared to countersteer—possibly several times—until you regain control.

- Do not use cruise control!

- If your front wheels start to skid, take your foot off the accelerator, and shift your vehicle to neutral. Don't steer the vehicle until you have slowed down and regained traction—then steer in the direction you want to go. Put the vehicle back in gear and slowly accelerate.

- If you get stuck, do not spin your wheels because you'll only dig your tires in deeper.

- To gain extra traction if you get stuck, place gravel, dirt, or sand in front of your tires and along your intended path.

- Bring along a set of snow chains. Even a four-wheel

>> Just don't let your vehicle get too deep in the snow—your differential doesn't make the greatest snow plow in the world. *Rick Shandley*

drive vehicle will handle better in snow with chains. Some states require chains or studded tires, even for four-wheel drive vehicles, under certain conditions (particularly on mountain roads). Other states prohibit the use of chains.

If you're planning to do some traveling in the white stuff, it's a good idea to bring the right kind of tires along with you—snow tires. True snow tires have a more aggressive tread than regular passenger car tires but not as aggressive as mud tires. This design allows snow to compress within the treads, creating more traction on the snowy surface. Snow tires also use a softer rubber in their manufacture, which offers better grip on snow and ice than the harder and longer-wearing rubber used for regular street tires. Check your local laws because some states also allow the use of special snow tires with metal studs, which are a must for driving on ice.

THE ICE THING

Remember, ice and snow are both freezing cold and both made of water but they act very differently from each other when you drive over them. While it's hard for people who haven't done much driving in snow to believe, snow can actually offer quite a bit of traction. It's no big deal for drivers to haul down an interstate highway at 50 or 60 miles an hour on snow. Of course, a good set of snow tires with an aggressive tread to grab on to the snow helps. And don't plan to hit your brakes and stop in the same distance as on dry pavement. It just won't happen.

Ice, however, is an entirely different animal than snow. Ice offers far less traction than snow—sometimes none at all. Anyone who has done any winter driving knows the deep feeling of helplessness you experience when you run across a patch of ice, hit your brakes, and keep right on going. The end result of the experience is often not a pretty one. You'll

>> **An aggressive all-terrain or snow tread will help you get through the white stuff.** *Rick Shandley*

keep going on your merry way until something else stops you, like a tree, or a curb, or another car. Ouch!

Whether you're planning to drive on ice or snow, you should practice on regular roads before you try the same moves off road. The next time it snows, find a big, empty school or shopping center parking lot and get a feel for how your rig feels when it's within the limits, and how it feels when it's almost ready to jump outside the limits. Practice driving on fresh snow, packed snow, and ice. Try starting out from a stop, and try stopping from a variety of different speeds. Be sure to make a lot of turns—starting out slow, then increasing your speed. Just make sure you don't hit any light poles or other cars! Before you know it, you'll be a pro on the snow and ice, and you'll be ready to take your act off road.

THE AMBASSADOR TO MEXICO

My close friend Frank Arciero Jr. tells a story about one trip we made together years ago. We were in Mexico, headed north to Mexicali after a race, and I decided to take a shortcut. Let's just say that the shortcut turned out to be anything but. I'll let Frank pick up the story from there: "We were driving to Mexicali where we would cross the border into Calexico on the U.S. side, then jump onto the interstate and zoom over to San Diego. But Ivan decided it would be better to stay in Mexico and cross the border at Tecate—about 90 miles to the west. This meant taking the brand-new Mexican highway that goes over the mountains between Tecate and Mexicali. In the wintertime, it can get icy and even snowy up there. Ivan said, 'Yeah, that will be a little faster for us.' I said, 'I don't think so, Ivan.' He said, 'Let's try it.' So that's what we did.

"We got into a little town called La Rumorosa at the top of mountain. The problem was, the locals had the highway blocked, and they weren't letting anyone go through. If we had to turn around, and headed back to Mexicali, we would have lost at least four or five hours—maybe more.

"So Ivan gets out—he knows a little Spanish—and he decides to become our ambassador. He just asked the protesters what was going on, and it turned out that the locals were all ticked off at the government and at the truckers, so they shut the highway down. They happened to be having a town hall meeting on the situation, and Ivan says to one of the guys who was involved, 'Listen, let me talk to the guys and I'll get our SCORE organization to see if we can (provide) some help through the government.' So the guy says, 'Okay.' The guy says something to the guys who are leading the protest. Then, he comes back and says, 'Okay, guys. Follow me.' We got in the truck and the guy led us through two or three little back roads—all the way around the roadblock and back on the highway on the other side. He said, 'Okay. Make sure you talk to your guy from SCORE and help us out,' and Ivan promised he would—and he did. We took off, and everybody else was still blocked up there. We would have been stuck up there for who knows how long if Ivan hadn't have been able to talk his way through that mess."

>> **Are we having fun yet?** *Rick Shandley*

... HILLS ARE THE ICING ON THE CAKE

chapter 15

>>UP
HILLS ...
AND DOWN<<

While you can have plenty of fun on the flats, taking your vehicle up and down hills is probably the icing on the cake of off-road adventures. There are, however, right and wrong ways to approach hills. Unless you're in a situation where you absolutely have to, you should avoid going sideways across a steep hill. It is way too easy to roll a vehicle if you cross the hill at too steep of an angle and lose control.

That said, if you do find yourself in this situation, and you have no other choice, the number one thing is to go slow—really slow, barely moving, lowest-gear-you've-got slow. What happens is that when you're moving along really slow, the weight of your vehicle stays low even when you hit bumps or ruts because your suspension absorbs the shocks. When you're going faster, however, the bumps overwhelm your suspension, and that pushes the weight of your entire vehicle up higher, making it more prone to tipping. As soon as you get the opportunity, turn your vehicle downhill and exit the situation.

I've done some testing to see what happens when you get a vehicle at too steep an angle going across a hill. I've had it right on the edge and beyond. Typically, a vehicle will slide before it will tip over. I even tried this in a paved canal one time, and my vehicle just slid instead of tipping over. Sliding is fine until you run into something that stops your vehicle, such as a rock, tree stump, or other obstacle. As soon as something gets in the way to stop your slide, you're going over.

So, again: Don't get yourself in that situation unless you absolutely have to, and if you have to, take it slow and be ready to turn downhill as soon as you possibly can.

GOING UP HILLS

Whenever you're dealing with hills, give them plenty of respect. Let me tell you, rolling down a hill is no fun. Take time up front to plan out a route with the least

161

PREVIOUS PAGE >> **Remember: It's often easier to get up a hill than it is to come back down. Keep that in mind when you're selecting your route.** *Rick Shandley*

amount of major obstacles such as deep ruts, holes, and loose or "crunchy" edges. Here are a few other things to keep in mind:

- Don't run out of horsepower halfway up the hill. Use your horsepower wisely and make it last by choosing the right gear or downshifting quickly if you start running out of steam.

- Keep in mind that choosing the right gear depends upon the amount of traction the surface will provide, the angle of the slope, the length of the ascent, and

the obstacles between you and the top. Focus on the hill, but keep your ears open—and the seat of your pants in tune—to the signs of a straining engine.

- If your vehicle wants to stop, then stop. If you run out of power or traction and begin to dig down, stop before you lose control and either dig yourself into a hole or twist your vehicle into a dangerous cross-hill position. Put the vehicle in reverse, and cautiously back down the hill for another go in a lower gear or on a different line.

>> **Climbing hills with a truck requires special care. Use a low gear, put the truck in four-wheel drive, and use as little speed as is required to make the grade. One of the challenges of climbing hills can be visibility. Roll down your window and look out to keep an eye on your line.** *Lee Klancher*

- Do not try to turn around on the hill. When in doubt, back down slowly and re-think your approach.

- Use basic common sense.

Remember, some hills are just too steep, and you can easily get into trouble if you wind up on something that you or your rig are not equipped to handle. While no absolute rule exists that can tell you in advance whether or not a hill is too steep, a number of different factors come into play. For example, a vehicle with a higher center of gravity is going to be more prone to rolling over on a steep hill than a vehicle with a lower center of gravity. Also, the surface of the trail up or down the hill plays a role. A slippery surface—sand, gravel, mud, icy snow—is more difficult to climb than a firm surface with lots of traction—sandstone, stable rocks, hard-packed dirt. The steepness of the hill itself plays a role as well. If you think it's too steep, it probably is.

GOING DOWN HILLS

While getting up a hill is half the fun, getting down again is the other half of the fun equation. Driving downhill can often be more dangerous and nerve-wracking than getting up in the first place. Once you've made it to the top of the hill, and you're safely over, stop and evaluate the situation again. Keep the following tips in mind:

- Plan your route down with the same care that you planned your route going up.

- Choose the appropriate gear. Let the engine do as much of the "braking" as possible, and be gentle on the brake pedal. Use a smooth throttle and keep your steering wheel in a neutral position.

- If the vehicle starts to "come around" on you, straighten the wheels downhill and accelerate slightly to bring the vehicle back in line—usually a light blip on the throttle is enough.

- Don't forget that as you drive downhill, weight is being transferred to the front end of your vehicle. When you brake, you transfer even more weight forward, and your rear axle will become very light. This

>> **Going down hills requires a similar approach to climbing. Use a low gear to reduce the strain on your brakes, and don't be afraid to look out the window to select a route for your front wheel.** *Lee Klancher*

means your vehicle's rear end can—and perhaps will—come around on you.

GOING ACROSS HILLS

As I pointed out at the beginning of the chapter, you should only drive across hills when you absolutely have to. Don't get into this habit! That said, when you do find yourself taking a side-hill route, here are a few tips that will improve the safety of your maneuver:

• Choose your route carefully, and always have an "escape plan" prepared in your head and line of sight.

• Choose your gearing.

• If the vehicle feels like it's starting to tip over, immediately point your front wheels down the hill and gently accelerate to bring the vehicle back in line.

THERE ARE A LOT OF HILLS (AND CLIFFS!) IN BAJA

I used to love racing in Baja in the middle of the night. You'd really have to keep your eyes open, though—a hard thing to do when you're tired from racing all day in the dirt, dust, and sun. There are some huge cliffs south of Bahía de los Ángeles where if you ever went off the side, they'd never find you— at least not that night. If you rolled down there and were hurt, you might never get out alive.

I was driving along and came across a couple of guys on BMW motorcycles. These were big touring bikes, and they were overloaded with gear. So, they started down a hill, not knowing exactly what they were getting into. They didn't realize how rough the road was going to get, but once they got a ways down the hill, they were committed. There was no turning back. Before you go down a hill, you've got to really think about why you're going downhill because you just might not be able to get back up. That was the case with these guys. They went past the point of no return, and then had to go through hell and back to get through the mess they soon found themselves in. The last I heard they made it through, but I don't know how they kept from burning up their clutches. I'm certain they thought twice the next time they had the "opportunity" to follow a trail downhill.

>> **Avoid driving across hills unless you've absolutely got to do it!** *Rick Shandley*

>> **Driving across a hill is a quick way to test your pucker factor!** *Rick Shandley*

>> **Be sure to keep an eye on your rear end when you're exiting the bottom of a hill. If your departure angle isn't high enough, you might get hung up.** *Rick Shandley*

PART 3

ULTIMATE TRAVEL ADVENTURE DESTINATIONS

Ready for travel adventure? In the following chapters, I offer my personal list of ultimate off-road travel adventure destinations. These are the places I go when I want to enjoy some good old-fashioned off-road adventure. Each short chapter contains a description of the destination, how to get there, where to stay, and a list of my favorite things to do and see.

...JUST COOL OFF AND RELAX.

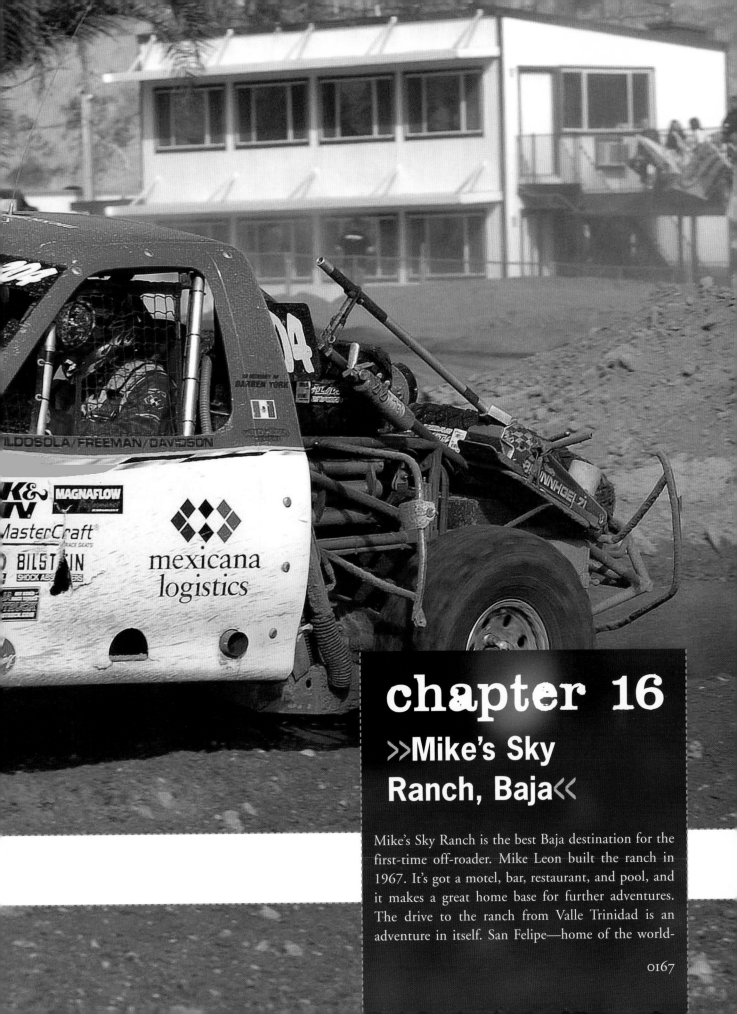

chapter 16
>>Mike's Sky Ranch, Baja<<

Mike's Sky Ranch is the best Baja destination for the first-time off-roader. Mike Leon built the ranch in 1967. It's got a motel, bar, restaurant, and pool, and it makes a great home base for further adventures. The drive to the ranch from Valle Trinidad is an adventure in itself. San Felipe—home of the world-

PREVIOUS PAGE >> **Routes that are legal to travel by off-road vehicles are usually clearly marked. Take the time to make yourself aware of local regulations.** *Lee Klancher*

famous fish taco—is not too far away to the southeast. Mike's is next to a large national park, and you can even go horseback riding, fishing, or hunting for deer, rabbit, and quail if you like. Or you can just cool off and relax.

WHERE IT'S AT

Mike's Sky Ranch is in Baja California, on the north side of the San Pedro Mártir National Park, approximately 100 miles southeast of Ensenada. Mike's Sky Ranch is located on a hill above the Arroyo San Rafael, which is a wooded valley flanked by steep mountains that include the Cerro San Matias, which rises to an altitude of 7,100 feet.

HOW TO GET THERE

From Ensenada, drive east 88 miles on Baja Highway 3. Turn right (south) at the large "Mike's Sky Ranch" sign, which you will see at about 11 miles past the town of Valle Trinidad. From the turnoff, proceed 19 miles along the well-marked dirt road to the entrance of Mike's Sky Ranch. The road starts out fairly smooth but gets rougher as it approaches the destination, so be sure your vehicle has adequate ground clearance—at least 10 inches or so. Most stock four-wheel drive trucks or SUVs should be fine. A regular car or truck? Maybe not. There are a few water crossings that are usually easy to get through, but that can become difficult in the event of heavy rains. If it is rainy or snowy, four-wheel drive would be a definite plus. There is also a 6,000-foot-long graded airstrip for private pilots to use. Try to plan your trip so you arrive during daylight hours and not at night. It gets very dark up in those Baja hills.

>> **Mike's Sky Ranch in Baja, California is one of the must-see off-road destinations. The roads around the ranch are classic Baja—rough, open, and threading through the mountains.** *Lee Klancher*

>> **Mike's Sky Ranch in Baja, California is one of the must-see off-road destinations. The roads around the ranch are classic Baja—rough, open, and threading through the mountains.** *Lee Klancher*

CHAPTER 3: THE OFF-ROAD ADVENTURER'S CODE

WHAT TO DO

- Relax, cool off, or warm up, depending on the season. Get a hearty meal and a good night's rest.

- Try one of Mike's famous margaritas.

- Fish in Mike's trout stream.

- Explore the nearby San Pedro Mártir National Park. The park contains many species of reptiles (such as rattlesnakes), amphibians, and fish. Numerous species of birds reside in the park as well as mammals, including rams, mule deer, coyotes, bobcats, gray foxes, rabbits, squirrels, and even mountain lions.

- Visit the National Astronomical Observatory in the highest part of San Pedro Mártir National Park (9,100 feet), operated by the National Autonomous University of Mexico (UNAM).

WHERE TO STAY

Unless you plan to camp out in the boonies, the ranch is your only option for overnight accommodations. Mike's offers 27 motel-type rooms ranging in price from about $25 to $45. An on-site restaurant serves breakfast, lunch, and dinner year round. You'll also find a swimming pool, small bar, large common room, and pool table. Campsites are also available along a nearby river. Be sure to make reservations well in advance, especially if you have a large group of off-roaders. Mike's is a popular place and can be booked up in advance, particularly on weekends.

FOR MORE INFORMATION

- Phone: 011-52 (664) 681-5514

>> **Mike's Sky Ranch has very simple accommodations, with a hotel with cheap rooms and a great meal served in the bar downstairs. The bar walls and ceiling are covered with signatures and business cards from everyone who's anyone in off-road riding and racing.** *Lee Klancher*

ONE DAY AT MIKE'S

Driving hundreds and hundreds of miles can get kind of boring sometimes even for professional racers. To help cure that boredom, we play a lot of practical jokes on friends, family, reporters, business associates, sponsors, and each other. One day, Frank Arciero, Jr. and I had finished having breakfast at Mike's Sky Ranch, and decided to go for a drive. I brought along a reporter in my vehicle, and Frank brought along his wife, Betty, in his vehicle. We drove out of Mike's and onto a graded road that goes up by the National Astronomical Observatory and meanders all the way down to Camalu, a popular surfing beach at the north end of the Bay of San Ramon on the Pacific Ocean.

I'll let Frank tell the story: "And so Ivan had the reporter, and I had Betty. Before we left Mike's, Ivan said, 'I'll bet you still remember that one section down there where if you make a hard left turn and go off the road, it looks like you're going off a cliff.' I replied, 'Yeah, I remember.' So Ivan says, 'Okay, I'll key you on the radio, and when I key you that means I'm going to go off the road there and see what this reporter does.' 'Oh, man,' I said, 'this guy's going to have a heart attack and I don't want to have to take him back to Ensenada to go to the hospital.'

"So we're motoring on down the road, and he keys his radio mike. Then, as he's going through a fast section, he made a hard left turn and ran right off the road. There's really a little shortcut there that goes to the next curve, but the passenger can't see it. From his point of view, it looks like they are going to make a 2,000-foot trip to the valley below. So Ivan jumps his truck off road and he yells, 'Aaaaaaaaah!' and that reporter, he was so scared and he was screaming so loud that I could hear him from half a mile back. Ivan scared the hell out of him. So my wife, Betty, asks, 'What's going on?' And I said, 'Honey, I don't know.' When I got to that little turnoff I did exactly the same thing Ivan did. I made the hard left and I yelled, 'Aaaaaaaaah!' She was so mad she slapped me and put two black-and-blue bruises on my shoulder."

NOW YOU'RE GETTING INTO A MORE SERIOUS

chapter 17

>>Gonzaga Bay, Baja<<

One of my favorite places in all of Baja is Gonzaga Bay. Now you're getting into a more serious off-road adventure. You're farther from the border, it's more desolate, and you won't be seeing any smooth, paved roads. What you'll be seeing are rough dirt roads. These roads, while passable by almost any vehicle, deter the casual tourist. If you persevere, you'll discover why I love Gonzaga. It's absolutely gorgeous and there are a wide variety of things to do when you get there. Of course, relaxing and enjoying the excellent food and refreshments is always near the top of my list of things to do.

WHERE IT'S AT

Gonzaga Bay (Bahia de Gonzaga in Spanish) is located on the Gulf of California (Sea of Cortez) approximately 100 miles south of San Felipe, and about 48 miles south of Puertecitos. The GPS coordinates are 29'48 latitude N ~ 114'23 longitude W.

HOW TO GET THERE

To get to Gonzaga Bay, drive south on the coast road approximately 48 miles from Puertocitos. One of the reasons that Gonzaga Bay is so pristine and beautiful is because it's not the easiest place in the world to get to. In fact, it can be downright difficult. The road south from Puertecitos has long had a reputation for being one of the worst roads in Baja. Despite the significant road grading provided by the Mexican government in the 1980s, this road is still very intimidating to all but the most seasoned Baja travelers. Regardless, any four-wheel drive vehicle and most two-wheel drive vehicles should be able to make it no problem. You might have a loose filling or two after you get there, but you will get there!

>> **A sleepy little resort known as Alfonsina's is the only place to stay in Gonzaga Bay. The food is decent, the rooms are rustic, and the sunsets make the price a steal.** *Lee Klancher*

WHAT TO DO

- Go fishing in the bay. There are plenty of grouper, bass, triggerfish, corvina, yellowtail, pompano, and barracuda waiting to be caught and cooked!

- Take the Gonzaga Bay Island tour; a relaxing sea cruise around the large island situated just off the coast is a wonderful way to soak in the natural beauty of Gonzaga Bay.

- Go snorkeling or scuba diving.

- Enjoy a kayaking expedition arranged by a local tour operator.

- Explore one of the many off-road trails in the area.

- Eat at one of the local restaurants, including Alfonsina's, the Punta Bufeo Restaurant, or the Gonzaga Bay Restaurant.

- Visit Coco's Corner—home of the famous Coco mentioned in chapter 1—just south of Gonzaga Bay.

WHERE TO STAY

- Alfonsina's Resort: Phone: 011-52 (664) 648-1951, Fax: 011-52 (664) 626-2626, E-mail address: alfonsinas@hotmail.com. Located near the end of the sand spit, at the north end of the dirt runway, east side, on the beach. Alfonsina's is the best place to stay when you visit Gonzaga Bay.

>>ABOUT THOSE PROPERTY LINES<<

In the United States, we do things by rights-of-way—property lines, power line rights-of-way, and so forth. Local roads generally have to respect those property lines, and they may zig this way and that between two points to do so. It doesn't work that way in Baja. In Baja, dirt roads between two points are laid out by the easiest way to get there, and they don't have property easements to worry about.

When I first started going down to Baja, I noticed that there would often be a "Y" in the road. We'd stop to try to figure out what was going on—which way should we go, left or right? So we stopped at maybe 15 of these divergent routes and got out the maps to figure it out. Of course, the maps didn't show them. Finally, we figured out what was going on. The reason there was a "Y" in the road was because a truck broke down right in the middle of the road and people started another road to get around it. Eventually the two separate routes would come back together.

It has 16 rooms, a restaurant, a bar, and a sun deck looking out over the Sea of Cortez. Rooms run $45 and sleep up to four people.

- Punta Bufeo Motel is located about three miles north of Gonzaga Bay in Punta Bufeo. There are only eight spartan rooms with cement floors and wood walls. Inexpensive, but not recommended unless Alfonsina's is all booked up.

FOR MORE INFORMATION

- www.bajaexpo.com/cities/gonzaga.htm

chapter 18

>>Moab, Utah<<

Moab, Utah, is the Mecca of the off-road world with over 30 trails to choose from, most within a short drive from town. These trails cover some of the most rugged and scenic country you will find anywhere. Forest, desert, steep sculptured canyon walls, rims, rivers, mountains, and famous Moab "slick rock" provide incredible variety and captivating beauty. Moab is close to a remarkable array of natural scenic wonders, including Arches National Park, Canyonlands National Park, the Colorado River, Dead Horse Point State Park, and more.

SEARCH FOR THE SITES...

WHERE IT'S AT

The town of Moab, Utah, is adjacent to Arches National Park, approximately 235 miles southeast of Salt Lake City, Utah, or 113 miles southwest of Grand Junction, Colorado.

HOW TO GET THERE

From Interstate 70 (which runs east-west from Grand Junction, Colorado, and points east, to its terminus at Interstate 15 in central Utah), take the US-191 exit (Exit 180) south. Continue 29 miles into the town of Moab.

WHAT TO DO

- Go mountain biking on one of the many well-marked and maintained trails in the Moab area.
- Go rafting on the Colorado River.
- Explore Arches National Park and Canyonlands National Park.
- Visit Native American petroglyph sites.
- Do some hiking, horseback riding, or off-roading in your vehicle.
- Search for the sites where major Hollywood movies such as Indiana Jones and the Last Crusade, City Slickers II, Mission Impossible II, and Thelma and Louise were filmed.
- Visit the Castle Creek or Spanish Valley wineries.
- Discover the Moab dinosaur tracks, including Allosaurus, Camptosaurus, Stegosaurus, and Camarasaurus.
- Explore the Anasazi cliff dwellings.

WHERE TO STAY

Choose from many different motel chains or independents—including Best Western, Comfort Suites, Days Inn, Holiday Inn, and locally owned hotels, motels, campsites, and bed and breakfasts. For a comprehensive listing—including rates and contact information—visit this website: www.discovermoab.com/hotels.htm.

FOR MORE INFORMATION

- www.discovermoab.com
- www.utah.com/moab
- www.moab-utah.com

>> **Moab is also a gorgeous destination, and a popular area to film movies.** *Thelma and Louise* **and** *Indiana Jones and the Last Crusade* **both used the area for location filming.** *Lee Klancher*

WELCOME TO THE VALLEY OF FIRE

chapter 19

>>Valley of Fire State Park, Nevada<<

Valley of Fire is Nevada's oldest state park. It was founded in 1935 and is located only 55 miles north-east of Las Vegas. The rough floor and jagged walls of the park are loaded with dirt roadways, sand dunes, hidden trails, and narrow red rock canyons great for off-road adventuring. The park contains brilliant formations of eroded sandstone and sand dunes more than 150 million years old. These features, which are the centerpiece of the park's attractions, often appear to be on fire when reflecting the sun's rays.

WHERE IT'S AT

The Valley of Fire State Park is located 6 miles northwest of Lake Mead and 55 miles northeast of Las Vegas.

HOW TO GET THERE

From Las Vegas, drive north on Interstate 15 approximately 35 miles to State Route 169. You will see a Paiute Indian Reservation Tobacco Shop and small casino at the exit. Drive east on Route 169 for approximately 15 miles until you reach the west entrance of the Valley of Fire State Park.

WHAT TO DO

- Find the petrified logs (but don't take any home).
- Explore for petroglyphs.
- Take photos of the remarkable sandstone formations.
- Check out the interesting rock formations, including the Beehives, Atl Atl Rock, the Silicon Dooms, and many more.
- Go fishing or boating in nearby Lake Mead.
- Tour Hoover Dam.
- Have some fun in Las Vegas.

WHERE TO STAY

An almost unlimited number of hotels and motels—at every price point possible—are available in nearby Las Vegas, Nevada. Whether you'd like to keep things low key—or jump in with both feet and make a big splash—you'll find that Las Vegas can easily meet your needs. Visit www.vegas.com for detailed information on Las Vegas accommodations.

For More Information

- http://parks.nv.gov/vf.htm
- www.desertusa.com/nvval
- http://en.wikipedia.org/wiki/Valley_of_Fire

>> **The sun sets in Valley of Fire State Park, which is 55 miles northeast of Las Vegas.** *Lee Klancher*

chapter 20

>>Assateague Island, Maryland/Virginia<<

Interested in an off-road adventure like no other? Then make your way to the beach on Assateague Island. Assateague Island National Seashore is located on one of the wildest stretches of barrier island remaining on the Atlantic Coast of the United States. Assateague Island has Maryland and Virginia off-road vehicle areas open year-round for off-road beach recreation. The Maryland portion of Assateague has an off-road vehicle zone 12 miles in length, with a 145-vehicle limit. Assateague offers a wilderness atmosphere on an ocean beach—a rare opportunity today, particularly along the crowded Atlantic seaboard.

WHERE IT'S AT

Assateague Island stretches for 37 miles along the coasts of Maryland and Virginia, bordered by the Atlantic Ocean to the east and the Sinepuxent and Chincoteague Bays to the west.

HOW TO GET THERE

There are two entrances to the island: Assateague's north entrance is at the end of Route 611, eight miles south of Ocean City, Maryland. The south entrance is at the end of Route 175, two miles from Chincoteague, Virginia. There is no vehicle access between the two entrances on Assateague Island.

WHAT TO DO

- See the famous Assateague wild ponies.
- Go swimming at the pristine beaches.
- Enjoy watching the many thousands of migratory birds that frequent the area.
- Go hiking on the numerous trails.
- Go canoeing or kayaking.
- Drive on the 12 miles of beach in Maryland and small section of beach in Virginia open to over-sand vehicles (OSV). It will cost you $70 to buy an annual OSV permit for the privilege.
- Go fishing, crabbing, or hunting for oysters.
- Visit the NASA Wallops Flight Facility and museum near Chincoteague, Virginia.
- Walk the boardwalk at Ocean City, Maryland.
- Enjoy eating some of Chincoteague's famous oysters.

WHERE TO STAY

Numerous lodging options are available at the north end of Assateague in Ocean City, Maryland, and at the south end of the island in Chincoteague, Virginia. Check out these websites for detailed information:

- Ocean City: www.assateagueisland.com/ocean_city/oc_hotel.htm
- Chincoteague: www.assateagueisland.com/chincoteague/hotels.htm

For More Information

- www.nps.gov/asis
- www.assateagueisland.com
- www.dnr.state.md.us/publiclands/eastern/assateague.html

...A WILDERNESS ATMOSPHERE ON AN OCEAN BEACH

chapter 21

>>Ocala National Forest, Florida<<

The Ocala National Forest offers many enjoyable locations for off-road vehicles. While the USDA Forest Service has not designated or marked specific ORV trails, there are plenty of unnumbered roads and travel ways zigzagging throughout the forest where you may ride. Restricted areas are designated to protect certain biological communities, such as wetlands.

ENJOY. TRAVEL. ZIGZAG.

PREVIOUS PAGE >>Ocala National Forest in Florida offers abundant opportunities for ORV use. The heavily-used forest is about 60 miles from Orlando. *Lee Klancher*

WHERE IT'S AT

The Ocala National Forest is located 3 miles east of Ocala, Florida; 16 miles southeast of Gainesville, Florida; and 18 miles northwest of Orlando, Florida.

HOW TO GET THERE

From Ocala, take Florida Highway 40 three miles east to the Visitor Center.

WHAT TO DO

- Go camping.
- Look for black bears and alligators.
- Explore the many off-road vehicle trails.
- Go mountain biking or horseback riding.
- Hike the Florida National Scenic Trail, Salt Springs Observation Trail, Lake Eaton Sinkhole Trail, St. Francis Trail, or Yearling Trail.
- Enjoy canoeing, kayaking, and boating.
- Go for a swim.
- Go hunting or fishing.

WHERE TO STAY

If you visit the Ocala National Forest, plan to camp. The park offers three classes of camping: developed campgrounds, primitive campsites, and dispersed tent camping. Developed campgrounds provide showers, restrooms, picnic tables, charcoal grills, fire rings, lantern holders, drinking water, sanitation facilities, and trash cans. Primitive campsites provide very limited facilities. Dispersed tent camping has no facilities or amenities at all. There are no fees for primitive or dispersed tent camping. Fees for developed campsites range from $4 to $22. A limited number of cabins are available at Lake Dorr and Sweetwater Spring. For additional information, visit: www.fs.fed.us/r8/florida/recreation/index_oca.shtml #camping. If you don't feel like roughing it, there are numerous lodging options available in Ocala, Gainesville, and Orlando.

FOR MORE INFORMATION

- www.fs.fed.us/r8/florida/recreation/index_oca.shtml
- http://gorp.away.com/gorp/resource/us_national_forest/fl_ocala.htm
- www.floridatrailriders.org/articles/ONF.htm

>> **The Ocala National Forest has made ORV use legal only on designated trails. Most trails are well-marked, but not all of them were as of February 2006.** *Lee Klancher*

chapter 22

>>Cape Cod, Massachusetts<<

If you love the seashore, and you love New England, it doesn't get better than Cape Cod. Situated at the southeastern corner of the state of Massachusetts, Cape Cod—simply known as "the Cape" by locals—offers a wide variety of both on- and off-road adventures. The jewel of Cape Cod (and the magnet for off-roaders) is the Cape Cod National Seashore. This park is made up of 43,604 acres of shoreline and upland landscape, lighthouses, historic structures, swimming beaches, nature trails, and picnic areas. There's plenty to do and see, and lots of opportunity for adventure.

If you get tired of all that adventure, you can always visit Boston—with the Cheers bar, Fenway Park, Quincy Market, the Boston Commons, Paul Revere's house, and a myriad of restaurants selling a lot of clam chowder. Life could be worse, right?

WHERE IT'S AT

Cape Cod is located at the southeastern corner of Massachusetts, and extends into the Atlantic Ocean due east of Boston.

HOW TO GET THERE

From Boston, follow Interstate 93 south, approximately 9 miles to the Route 3 south off ramp and continue for 43 miles until you arrive in Sandwich, the gateway to Cape Cod from the north.

WHAT TO DO

- Swim.
- Surf.
- Sun.
- Fish.
- Dig for clams.
- Drive on the beach.
- Check out the lighthouses.
- Eat clam chowder and local lobsters.
- Visit Boston, Nantucket, or Martha's Vineyard.

WHERE TO STAY

There are many, many lodging options in Cape Cod. Here is a good place to look: www.capecodchamber.org.

FOR MORE INFORMATION

- www.nps.gov/caco
- www.capecodonline.com
- www.capecod.com

VARIETY OF BOTH ON- AND OFF-ROAD ADVENTURES.

chapter 23

>>Jeep Jamobree<<

The Jeep Jamboree is not a specific destination. It is an organization that sponsors off-road events of various degrees of difficulty across the country. However, as the name indicates, only Jeeps are invited to participate. If you don't have one, you'll need to rent or borrow one from a friend.

WHERE IT'S AT
Although destinations change from year to year, the 2007 Jeep Jamboree schedule includes adventures in:
- Oak Ridge, Tennessee
- Moab, Utah
- Hot Springs, Arkansas
- Catskill Mountains, New York
- Amarillo, Texas
- Ouray, Colorado
- Canyon de Chelly, Arizona
- Pine Barrens, New Jersey
- Snowshoe Mountain, West Virginia

HOW TO GET THERE
The Jeep Jamboree organizers will send you a complete registration package—mailed six to eight weeks prior to the event—that includes directions to your destination.

WHAT TO DO
It's all Jeep, all the time.

WHERE TO STAY
Lodging options will also vary depending on your destination. Your registration packet will include a list of motels, campgrounds, and RV accommodations in the area of the Jeep Jamboree you select.

FOR MORE INFORMATION
- www.jeepjamboreeusa.com
- www.jeep.com/jeep_life/events/jamborees/index.html

JEEP ONLY.

chapter 24

>>The Rubican Trail, California<<

The Rubicon Trail is justifiably considered by many to be the ultimate off-road adventure destination, and it's not for the faint of heart. The 22-mile-long trail rates a solid 10 in difficulty, and the trail has eaten alive many vehicles—and their drivers! Officially the Rubicon Trail is a non-maintained county road through Placer and El Dorado Counties, and it is surrounded by private land and USDA Forest Service property.

The Rubicon Trail—dubbed the "crown jewel of all off-highway trails"—is the premiere off-road vehicle route in the United States. The trail has narrow passages, rocky climbs, and mud holes. The names of some of the most famous obstacles will give you some indication of what drivers on the trail face: Spillway, Gatekeeper, Granite Bowl (Slabs), Soup Bowl, Little Sluice, Old Sluice, Big Sluice, and Rubicon Springs. Locals recommend bringing along a short-wheelbase vehicle with a full set of skid plates. I recommend you bring along a good insurance policy.

WHERE IT'S AT
The Rubicon is located in the Sierra Nevada Mountains of northeastern California between Lake Tahoe and Georgetown Lake approximately 80 miles east of Sacramento and 35 miles east of Placerville.

HOW TO GET THERE
To drive the trail from east to west—the usual approach—you'll start your journey at Loon Lake. To get there, take Highway 50 east out of Placerville about 20 miles until you arrive at the Ice House Road/Crystal Basin exit where you will turn off the main highway. Follow Ice House Road for approximately 28 miles to the intersection of Loon Lake Road, which goes to the right. Follow it four miles more to the second Loon Lake dam. This is the beginning of the Rubicon Trail.

WHAT TO DO
- Drive the Rubicon Trail.
- Watch others drive the Rubicon Trail—well worth the price of admission!
- Explore the Gold Rush country.
- Visit beautiful Lake Tahoe.
- Go gambling in Reno, Nevada.
- Ski or mountain bike at one of the many resorts in the surrounding mountains.

WHERE TO STAY
If you decide to drive the Rubicon Trail—a process that usually takes from two to three days—you'll be sleeping in a tent near the trail. However, when you first arrive or have completed your adventure, there are two lodging options not far from the Rubicon Trail head: the Ice House Resort and Robbs Valley Resort.

- The Ice House Resort is located at an altitude of 5,400 feet, and the resort is open from May 15 through October 15. There are 32 individual campsites ($15/night), a group campsite ($150/night for up to 50 people), five motel rooms ($72 to $88/night), a general store, and a full-service restaurant and bar. The resort is situated on a lake and it offers ample boating and fishing opportunities. Phone: (530) 293-3321, website: www.icehouseresort.com
- Robbs Valley Resort is in the process of converting from a campground and RV resort to one that also offers lodging. To this end, the owners have built two private cabins and five bunkhouse cabins. More are in the works. The resort also offers a general store, restaurant, and bar, and is open from spring through fall. Phone: (866) 978-5824, website: www.dorobbs.com

FOR MORE INFORMATION
- www.delalbright.com/rubicon/rubicon.htm
- www.rubicon-trail.com
- www.rubicontrail.org

About Ivan "Ironman" Stewart

Ivan "Ironman" Stewart is one of the most famous and highly visible automobile racers of all time. He's a living legend in off-road racing. He has made the nickname "Ironman" a reality by successfully overcoming off-road racing's toughest obstacles throughout his 28-year career, winning again and again.

Stewart's racing career was jump-started in 1973 when he was called to pilot a Class 2 buggy when his co-driver at the Ensenada 300 broke his leg before the race. It was the first of many solo victories that resulted in the nickname "Ironman" and, eventually, to a partnership with Toyota in 1983—a collaboration that has created unprecedented success that continues to this day.

Toyota and Ivan Stewart reached victory immediately in desert and stadium off-road racing. During the 12-year history of the Mickey Thompson Entertainment Group (MTEG) stadium series, Toyota earned 11 manufacturers' championships and 42 main event victories—nearly three times more than any other truck team. Stewart holds the record for all-time MTEG wins with 17 victories. In the desert, Stewart has accumulated 84 career victories and 10 driver's championships. The wins include 17 Baja 500s, eight Mint 400s, four Parker 400s, three Baja 1,000s, and four SCORE World Championships.

>>IVAN "IRONMAN" STEWART CAREER HIGHLIGHTS<<

- 84 Career Victories
- 10 Career Driver's Championships
- 17 Baja 500 Wins
- 3 Baja 1000 Wins
- 8 Mint 400 Wins
- 4 Parker 400 Wins
- 4 SCORE Off-Road Championships
- 42 Mickey Thompson Stadium Main Event Wins
- 10 Mickey Thompson Driver's Championships

Ironman's success and popularity led to Off-Road Challenge, an extremely popular video and arcade game based on Stewart's participation in the SCORE Desert Series, and an off-road virtual reality experience at the Sahara Hotel in Las Vegas. Stewart has also been a featured participant in the Toyota Pro/Celebrity Race and the Pikes Peak International Hill Climb "Challenge of Champions." Stewart plays an active role in the community, working with a variety of nonprofit organizations, including the Special Olympics and the Make-A-Wish Foundation. Ironman adopted a school for the deaf in Ensenada, Mexico, where he regularly visits and assists in fund raising.

index

2x4, 14, 15

4x4, 9, 14, 16, 17

Altitude, 93

Angle of approach, 9, 22, 23

Angle of departure, 23, 25

Anticipating, 34

Antilock braking system (ABS), 90

Arciero, Frank Jr., 10, 11, 159

Assateague Island,
    Maryland/Virginia, 183

Attitude, 64

Bahia de los Angeles, 10

Baja, 10, 11, 18, 43, 52, 81, 112,
    122, 164

Baja 1000, 10, 45, 55, 88, 89, 97,
    103, 113

Baja 500, 45, 55, 103, 113, 116

Baja Protruck Racing, 16, 80

Battery, 46

Blankets, 31

Blind spot, 129

Body lift, 25

Booby traps, 152

Boulders, 25, 149

Boundaries, 51

Braking techniques, 89

Braking techniques, Emergency,
    103, 104

Breakover angle, 19, 25

Broken parts, 64

Buddies, 41, 51

Call of nature, 146

Cape Cod, Massachusetts, 186

Catching air, 88

CB radio, 35

Cell phone, 31, 35, 39

Checklist, 45, 46

Chevy Trailblazer, 23

Chugach Mountain Range,
    Alaska, 126

Clearances, 25, 150, 153

Cliffs, 164

Climate, 20

Coco's Corner, 10, 18

Comfort zone, 73

Common sense, 78

Concentration, 46

Corral, Charlotte, 70, 88

Course, Plotting, 153

Cruise control, 157

Dalton, Highway, Alaska, 129

Damage, 44

Desert, 31

Destinations, 37, 165
    Choosing, 19, 20
    Recommendations, 19

Differential, 59, 104, 150, 157
    Limited-slip (LSD), 17
    Locking, 17, 18, 145
    Open, 17

Dirt, 111

Discipline, 103

Driver responsibility, 86

Dust, 111

Dust cloud, 116

El Cajon, California, 73

El Mirage, 137

Engine belts, 46

Ensenada, 70

Ensenada 300, 93

Environment, 51

Estes Park, Colorado, 132

Eye positioning, 100

Eye techniques, 89

First-aid kit, 32, 37, 38

Fish, Sal, 70

Flashlight, 40

Fluid levels, 46

FM radio, 33, 35

Fog, 68

Ford Bronco, 103

Formula 1, 14

Four-wheel drive (4WD), 36, 43,
    101, 153
    Automatic, 15
    Full-time, 15
    Part-time, 15

Front wheel lock-up, 90

Gear choice, 90, 93, 137, 145, 156

Global positioning system (GPS),
    32, 36, 38, 40

Goals, 32, 51

Gonzaga Bay, Baja, 10, 122, 174–177

Ground clearance, 19, 22, 23

Habitats, Sensitive, 60

Hazards, 100, 117

Helping, 50, 51

Hill climbing, 45

Hills, 16, 22, 23, 25, 58, 61, 82, 161
    Going across, 164
    Going down, 163
    Going up, 161–163

Hrynko, Bill, 93, 96

Hummer, 17, 29

H1, 23, 25

Ice, 81, 93, 155

Indianapolis 500, 14

Ironman name, 55

Jeep Jamboree, 187

Jeep Wrangler, 17

Jenner, Bruce, 129

Johnson, John, 122

Johnson, Johnny, 10, 11

Jones, Parnelli, 43, 103

Jumper cables, 40

Jumps, 152

La Paz, 52, 70, 89, 97

Leadville, Colorado, 12

Lighting, 108

Limits, 20, 22, 29, 58, 60, 65, 93
    Vehicle, 82, 88

Line of sight, 100

Locations, 10